Florence Erickson
from
Mattilde Hjermstad

God bless you, dear Florence.

Sept 3rd 1939.

PIONEERING FOR CHRIST
IN THE SUDAN

Pioneering for Christ in the Sudan

· By ·

Johanna Veenstra
(Sudan United Mission)

Seventh Thousand

SMITTER BOOK COMPANY
Publishers
GRAND RAPIDS, MICH., U. S. A.

DEDICATED

TO THE MEMORY OF
MY BELOVED FATHER

THE LATE REV. WILLIAM VEENSTRA

(1868—1902)

Johanna Veenstra

PREFACE

WHEN coming home for this second furlough, there was not even a remote desire in my heart to write a book and tell of my experiences during five years of service in the Dark Continent. I have never thought myself capable of performing such a task; and even now I hesitate to set this work before the public.

One day this summer our kind Director of Missions, Dr. H. Beets (Christian Reformed Church), approached me on this subject of writing a book. At first his suggestion made no impression whatsoever upon my mind. Later on I was confronted with the fact that I was compelled to refuse many invitations to speak in the different churches and tell of the Lord's work in the Sudan. For lack of time it became impossible to travel about in so many states of the Union and in Canada, to reach all the people interested in the spread of the gospel in this needy field. A physical complication—overstrain of the vocal cords—also forced me to limit the amount of speaking appointments.

Then I began to pray about the matter of writing a book, so that all who are interested in the work, the problems, and the fruit of the gospel message among the Dzompere, a cannibal tribe in Central Africa whereunto the Lord has called me, might have opportunity to know the facts. It seemed more and more clear that I was to heed the suggestion of Dr. Beets, and give a part of my furlough time to writing this book on the experiences of "Pioneering for Christ" in the land of Ethiopia.

However much I have disliked the use of the personal pronoun, it seems there is no way of avoiding it. It is a help to know that in Scripture we find God's messengers frequently referring to themselves and using the personal pronoun.

It would be out of place for me to pose as an authority on missionary problems, missionary strategy, etc. An experience of five years is too inadequate to permit one giving a theoretical treatise on missionary effort. This book is meant to be an appeal for lives and for intercession. I do not claim that the book possesses any literary merit. If it has attraction, the honor is due to our Lord and the sufficiency of His grace.

It is my sincere hope that those who read these pages may be led to praise God that even among the cannibal people of Central Africa His promise is being fulfilled: "I will call them my people which were not my people; and her beloved, which was not beloved. And it shall come to pass in the place where it was said unto them, Ye are not my people; there shall they be called the children of the living God."

Further, that those who know what it means to wrestle with the Almighty in prevailing intercession may be led to pray for the converts, the missionaries, and the many tribes still untouched. Then shall we see fulfilled the word of the Lord, "Ethiopia shall soon stretch out her hands unto God."

JOHANNA VEENSTRA.

Ibi-via Jos-
Northern Nigeria
British West Africa
October, 1926

CONTENTS

Chapter		Page
I.	Farewell	23
II.	The Call to Service..............................	29
III.	Preparation for Service—I.......................	37
IV.	Preparation for Service—II......................	47
V.	"In Journeyings Often . . ."	55
VI.	The Call of the Sudan...........................	71
VII.	Getting Acquainted	77
VIII.	Entering the Cannibal District	83
IX.	The Power of Spirit Worship....................	93
X.	The Moral Life of the Dzompere	101
XI.	"In Perils in the Wilderness"—I	107
XII.	"In Perils in the Wilderness"—II.................	115
XIII.	The Task of a Pioneer Missionary................	123
XIV.	The Dispensary Work at Lupwe..................	129
XV.	The Boarding School at Lupwe...................	139
XVI.	Evangelistic Work	153
XVII.	First Fruits	175
XVIII.	The First Convert from among the Dzompere.......	187
XIX.	"Suffer the Little Children to Come"..............	199
XX.	A Few Questions Answered......................	207
XXI.	Problems and Difficulties.......................	219
XXII.	"Is It Nothing to You?"..........................	231

LIST OF ILLUSTRATIONS

Page

Miss Johanna Veenstra.................................. 10

Map showing Miss Veenstra's station..................... 20

The Mauretania 24

The author's home 26

Just as they are 34

Boarding school pupils exercising........................ 44

Tapping wine from the palm tree........................ 52

Map showing mission stations in the Sudan..............56, 57

The barge in which author spent fourteen days........... 62

"First fruits" of the gospel 66

Boarding school pupils in school dress................... 68

Group of Lupwe boarding school pupils.................. 74

A group of Dzomperes................................... 87

Spirit hut 96

Two Christian lads with patient and child wife........... 102

African buffalo 118

Leopard in the wilderness............................... 124

Hippopotamus 126

Boarding school pupils in their Sunday clothes........... 140

Compound of boarding school pupils..................... 145

Native Christians on preaching tour..................... 154

Pa'ana, "The Daughter of Prayer"....................... 160

Takum women going to the hill for palm wine........... 172

African monkeys 196

Helping the missionary 204

Python and leopard in life and death struggle........... 216

Baby of boarding school 228

"Separate me Barnabas and Saul for the work whereunto I have called them."

ACTS 13:2.

The Holy Spirit, as the representative of the ascended Lord, is supreme in the Church. It is His sovereign voice that summons His chosen workers to undertake missionary or home enterprise. Dr. Ryland, who at first opposed Carey's idea of going to India, said afterwards, "I believe God Himself infused into the mind of Carey that solicitude for the salvation of the heathen which cannot be fairly traced to any other source." And the same is true of all missionaries. The true call is always of the Divine Spirit. Whom He wills to call, He calls. Whom He calls, He separates. Whom He separates, He endows and sends forth.

F. B. MEYER.

INTRODUCTION

AFRICA looms increasingly large on the horizon of missionary interest. From September 14-20, 1926, at Le Zoute, in Belgium, an international conference was held to study the rapidly changing and developing conditions in the various parts of that great continent, and trying to discover how the missionary forces might effectively relate themselves to these conditions, in order to more rapidly advance the interests of the Kingdom of God.

Not less than thirteen countries were represented at that meeting, and sixty-three missionary societies from Europe, America and South America as well as from Africa contributed to its personnel. And well might this interest be shown in such a manner. As to evangelical mission work, Africa as well as South America may well be termed a *neglected* continent. Stanley in his days spoke of it as "The Dark Continent." This name, too, is fitting; and that not alone because its one hundred and fifty million or more inhabitants (except about two million whites) are dark skinned people; but also and especially because these multitudes have during many, many centuries been living in moral and spiritual darkness, under the sway of the Prince of Darkness. Theirs has been an existence full of intellectual darkness as well. Of the 523 distinct languages and 320 dialects which so far have been identified in Africa, great numbers have not yet been reduced to writing. That means ignorance and the offspring of ignorance: immorality, witchcraft and idolatry; degradation in a thousand ways; the oppression of the poor, the weak and the helpless—and the future full of gloom.

In recent decades Africa has been pictured as a great question mark: its shape suggesting this—a great question mark as to its pagan population of some eighty or ninety millions of people becoming either Mohammedan or Christian—since paganism is bound to disappear before the onward march of civilization, in quest of the treasures hidden in the soil, the forests and the mines of Africa. From the north, Islam has been forging ahead with rapids strides, its every trader a missionary; and the demands of its religion pleasing to the flesh and at the same time offering happiness for eternity. From the south, missionary bands of evangelical Christendom have been marching northward, alas, at a slow pace and in but small numbers, and these often depleted by the ravages of the climate and obstructed in their march by bitter foes, both black and white.

In different parts of Africa, notably in Uganda and the Kameruns, encouraging victories have been won for the Christ. But vast regions are yet without heralds of the gospel. The Sudan, the immense region south of the Sahara, has become a battlefield between Cross and Crescent. It is in that vast belt of dark, if not darkest, Africa, that the Sudan United Mission has since 1904 been endeavoring to establish a chain of mission posts, to halt, with God's help, the forward march of Mohammedanism; by having its soldiers of the Cross endeavor to conquer the pagan tribes of the country before they become the prey of Islam.

The Sudan United Mission has five councils, viz.: in England, Denmark, Australia, South Africa and the United States, the last named branch having its headquarters at Camden, N. J. It is under the auspices of the American branch that the author of the present volume has been laboring in recent years, supported by funds, coming largely from the people in America among whom she was reared; and pioneering for Christ in loyalty to the great principles of the denomination of which her father was an honored minister.

How the Lord of her life providentially prepared her for her work; pointed out the sphere of her labors; what she observed,

encountered and did in a part of the great mission field of the
Nigerian Sudan; and what its great problems and difficulties are—
Miss Veenstra tells in a straightforward, plain, informing and
interesting way. The great purpose of her book is, as she writes,
to appeal for lives and for intercession for Dark Africa, that it
increasingly may come to know Him who is the Light of the
World. We trust the volume, no doubt written with the heart
uplifted to the God of all grace, will be honored by Him to have
his Kingdom come also among the sons and daughters of the land
of Ham.

HENRY BEETS.

Grand Rapids, Mich., November 1, 1926.

MISSION STATIONS IN NORTHERN NIGERIA.

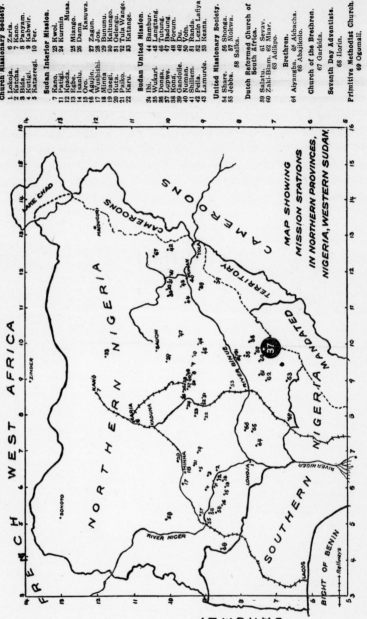

Church Missionary Society.
1. Lokoja.
2. Ketcha.
3. Bida.
4. Kutigi.
5. Kataeeregi.
6 Zaria.
7 Kano.
8 Panyam.
9 Kabwir.
10 Per.

Sudan Interior Mission.
7. Kano.
11 Patigi.
12 Kpada.
13 Egbe.
14 Isanlu.
15 Oro.
16 Aguin.
17 Wushishi.
18 Minna.
19 Gaegi.
20 Kuta.
21 Paiko.
22 Karu.
23 Kwrol.
24 Kurmin Musa.
25 Mlango.
26 Danna.
Kasuwa.
27 Zagun.
28 Jos.
29 Bununu.
30 Kaltungo.
31 Gelengu.
92 Tula Wange.
83 Katange.

Sudan United Mission.
34 Ibi.
35 Wukari.
36 Donga.
37 Lupwe.
38 Kona.
39 Gandolie.
40 Numan.
41 Shileim
42 Pela.
43 Lamurde.
44 Bambur.
45 Langtang.
46 Tutung.
47 Badung.
48 Forum.
49 Du.
50 Vom.
51 Randa.
52 Kilba Lafiya
53 Keana.

United Missionary Society.
54 Share.
55 Jebba.
56 Shonga.
57 Mokwa.
58 Salka.

Dutch Reformed Church of South Africa.
59 Salatu.
60 Zaki-Biam.
61 Sevav.
62 Mkar.
63 Adikpo.

Brethren.
64 Aiyangba.
65 Akbacha.
66 Abajikolo.

Church of the Brethren.
67 Garkida.

Seventh Day Adventists.
68 Ilorin.

Primitive Methodist Church.
69 Ogumali.

MAP SHOWING
MISSION STATIONS
IN NORTHERN PROVINCES,
NIGERIA, WESTERN SUDAN.

Number 37 is Miss Veenstra's station. See page 77.

CHAPTER I

"*Go ye into all the world, and preach the Gospel to every creature.*"

"*. . . Depart; for I will send thee far hence unto the Gentiles.*"

"*Be strong and of a good courage; be not afraid, neither be thou dismayed: for the Lord thy God is with thee whithersoever thou goest.*"

CHAPTER I

FAREWELL

"This is positively the last call! All people not traveling must leave the ship at once."

Through every passageway, and on every deck, we could hear the voice of an Englishman bidding passengers to say a last farewell to their friends and send them off the vessel.

Some people were traveling alone. They paid no attention to this call. Others, having crossed the "great deep" many times before, gave their friends a quick, hearty handshake, thus bidding them a cheerful good-bye. But some were suffering real grief—that painful parting that is accompanied by a fearful uncertainty as to whether they would ever see one another again. A long loving embrace—an affectionate kiss—tears—one last tender word—and a group of friends and loved ones file in procession down the gangplank to join the crowd that is waiting on the pier. Only a limited number are allowed a pass to board the ship and see their friends off, but by far the great majority have to be content with standing on the pier and watching the vessel move out.

It was one of those cold, rainy, cheerless days in October, exactly seven years ago today, October 2nd.

The ship was that large trans-Atlantic liner, the "Mauretania," used so much during the war for the transportation of troops and Red Cross workers. For this trip the vessel had a full enrollment. It was crowded to its utmost capacity with passengers.

So it was not a little handful of people that thronged all the available deck space. Each person wanted to be near the railing, so as to get a full view of his or her friends as they waited on the pier below.

"How long it takes for the boat to start," a passenger said. Then another, "My, but it's cold and damp. We shall all be sick." But for the most part the people were very quiet.

Suddenly from the pier below there came the sound of a beautiful hymn,

"Anywhere with Jesus I can safely go."

We could see hundreds of people on the pier below cast a glance at the group of Christians singing the hymn. And on

Courtesy of Cunard Line
The Mauretania. See page 23.

each deck the passengers looked all about them to see whether there was a Salvation Army cap or bonnet. They were all inquisitive to know the reason for this singing, and who the passengers were receiving this strange farewell. Then suddenly came the strains of a more familiar hymn,

"God be with you 'till we meet again."

A lady standing beside me was intensely moved. She looked at me and said, "Why, I believe surely, they are singing for you."

And I quietly assured her that she was right. Then she asked me if this was the first time I was traveling, and I said, "This is my first ocean journey; I am traveling alone, and am on my way to Africa as missionary." At once she began to weep and say, "I thought it must be something like that. The singing is lovely. It makes me sad because I have just buried a daughter, a very lovely young girl. I would like for us to have a talk before we get to England."

By this time all the heavy ropes that held the big vessel in place were loosened; and the tiny tugboats began to puff and pull with all their strength. Gradually they pulled the monstrous vessel out of her slip and into the broad waters of the Hudson River.

Handkerchiefs were waving—hundreds of them. What tense excitement! But through all the excitement one could hear the last hymn,

"Take the Name of Jesus with you."

The lone missionary stood on the deck, just at the railing, with a New Testament lifted high, while the choir of loving friends could still be heard to sing,

"Precious Name, O how sweet,
Hope of earth, and joy of heaven.

"At the name of Jesus bowing,
Falling prostrate at His feet;
King of kings, in heaven we'll crown Him,
When our journey is complete."

"Be it ever so humble, there's no place like home." Two round mud huts, 20 feet in diameter, covered with one grass roof—affording veranda space between the huts. This is the home of the author. See page 86.

CHAPTER II

Take my life, and let it be
Consecrated, Lord, to Thee;
Take my moments and my days,
Let them flow in ceaseless praise.

Take my hands, and let them move
At the impulse of Thy love;
Take my feet and let them be
Swift and beautiful for Thee.

Take my voice and let me sing
Always, only, for my King;
Take my lips and let them be
Filled with messages from Thee.

Take my silver and my gold;
Not a mite would I withhold;
Take my intellect and use
Ev'ry power as Thou shalt choose.

Take my will, and make it Thine;
It shall be no longer mine.
Take my heart, it is Thine own;
It shall be Thy royal Throne.

Take my love, my Lord, I pour
At Thy feet its treasure-store;
Take myself, and I will be
Ever, only, ALL for THEE.

FRANCES HAVERGAL.

CHAPTER II

THE CALL TO SERVICE

"Just how were you called to the mission field?"

This is a question many kind friends have ventured to ask me. It is not an easy matter to explain, and calls us to step back a few years and recall some of the outstanding experiences which led to a definite "call" to the Lord's service.

Let me say that to relate one's spiritual experiences reminds me of the Tabernacle. You remember its divisions: the *outer court,* the *holy place,* and the *holy of holies.*

So in our spiritual life there is what I may compare with the "outer court." That part of us—what we *say* and what we *do*— that is known to all those about us.

But behind our practical Christian living is the deeper life that I would compare with the "holy place." There is only a limited circle of friends who are invited to "come and hear what the Lord has done for my soul." We tell of answered prayer; of communion with our Lord; of battles fought and victories won in our soul-life.

Then there is that sacred part of our spiritual experience that I would liken to the "holy of holies." Before crossing the border into that place, one would surely whisper, "Take the shoes from off thy feet, for this is hallowed ground." It is hard to lift the veil and let one have a glimpse of that inner life. To tell of His gracious leading when drawn, laden with sin, to Calvary's cross; to tell how His voice was heard to say, "Go, work in my vineyard"; to tell of His soothing comfort in the hour of great sorrow; to tell of those rare mountain-top experiences of spiritual joy—is like reverently entering the "holy of holies."

And still I feel urged to give a few details of my own spiritual experiences in order that some may thereby, perchance, receive help and blessing.

* * * * * * * *

As a little girl, I was very naughty. In mischief I would easily have gained first prize in school and also in church. To this day it is a great sorrow to me to think back upon that time; and with the psalmist I may well pray, "Remember not, O Lord, the sins of my youth." I will not enlarge upon these sins, but to convince you of the truth of what I am saying, I might tell you that I was publicly expelled from Sunday School when only thirteen years of age. In catechism class we decided to tease our leader (not a minister) and I was to have a mock fainting spell. This was carried out and five of us girls were allowed to leave the room. I remember one outstanding week in day school when I was sent to appear before the principal three times. All this was before my fourteenth birthday.

Not long after my fourteenth birthday I was working in a New York office. Having passed the required examination in stenography I soon obtained a position, but this necessitated my going to and fro from Paterson to New York each day.

At that time New York was the second largest city in the world. A city with a tremendous foreign population; a city of extreme contrasts. There were high towering office buildings, and not far away were congested slums; there was the rich Wall Street section of the downtown district, but nearby were to be found the poorest of the poor; there was Riverside Drive with its palatial homes, but not far off were tenement houses where whole families were crowded into one tiny room. There were magnificent churches where folks came to worship, dressed in costly garments and riding in luxurious automobiles, and over on the other side of the island was the Bowery and Chinatown with its mission halls, where men and women, deceived by rum and opium, would come for rest, free lunch, free bed, work, and the cheer of a warm lighted room with its gospel songs and message. There was a very exclusive class of society folk called "the 400"; and there was what is commonly known as "New York's underworld," where hundreds of young lives have been wrecked, body and soul, in a cesspool of wickedness.

And into this great city, I a young girl of fourteen, went to work as a stenographer.

All the other girls had pretty clothes. I was earning a good salary, and also wanted beautiful clothes and jewelry. Other girls went to the "pictures," and it did not require much persuasion to get me along. Next in order was the theater, and soon I sat there in the midst of a great crowd. From the theater to the dance hall is only a single step, and I was prepared to take this step also. I had one lesson in dancing—and then God spoke, "Thus far and no farther"; and sent His Holy Spirit into my heart to slay me with conviction.

I do not mean to preach to anyone in this little book. But I feel quite certain that some of our young people will be reading these pages. And while there is such a tendency in our day to be broadminded, and while many seem to walk freely upon the paths that were formerly forbidden, may I, from my own personal experience, warn you to keep away from places of worldly amusements.

* * * * * * * *

"Come now, and let us reason together, saith the Lord: though your sins be as scarlet, they shall be as white as snow; though they be red like crimson, they shall be as wool."

It is only fitting that at this time I should bear testimony to the faithful personal work of the late Rev. K. Van Goor, who was my pastor at this time. How well do I remember his counsel and his pleading prayers. To this day I believe that personal work is Scriptural (e.g., Jesus dealing with Nicodemus, and Jesus dealing with the woman at the well); and that personal work is very fruitful. Away out in Africa I have spent hours in just this kind of work, dealing with the individual in regard to his or her soul-welfare. True, it is very difficult. Surely every Christian worker will find it easier to talk to a small group or to a large crowd than to just one person. But it is exactly the hard things in life that are so worth while. And to prove what I said regarding the pastor, the late Rev. Van Goor, I will go just a little into detail, in the hope that some may be encouraged in this great work of dealing with the individual.

One evening the telephone rang. It was for me. And the person speaking was the "dominee." He asked whether I had time that evening to come to his house for a little talk. I answered "Yes," and soon was on my way. As I rang the bell I felt myself shake with nervousness. But his kindly voice and manner soon brought me back to normal. He asked me many questions, and then he began to probe into my heart-life. I wept and confessed to him that I had "no peace in my soul." He talked some more, and then prayed with me, and I returned home.

Then on several occasions he would ask my chum and me to stay for a little talk after catechism. My chum was also undergoing a spiritual struggle, and so he could speak to us together. He never asked one of us to remain alone. These were precious moments. He never kept us long. Just having had the catechism lesson, our minds were in a proper attitude to receive a direct approach. A few questions, some more advice, an earnest prayer, and we were free to go home.

By this time I was earnestly seeking the Lord, but had no peace. For nearly a year I struggled under constant pressure of conviction. What a load of sin! Was it too late? Had the "unpardonable sin" been committed? Others sang, "What a wonderful Savior is Jesus my Lord, He taketh my burden away"—would I never know the joy of singing these words? Long into the night would I keep awake, sometimes reading the Bible, afraid to go to sleep—lest I might die. Months went by; words became fewer; and physically the strain was beginning to tell. But why all this struggle? The Holy Spirit made it clear to me. I wanted peace, but in my own way. I was very willing, more than willing, to give my *heart* to the Lord, but I shrank from giving my *all*. I wanted to be a child of the King, but I fought desperately against consecrating my *life* unto the service of that King! But who was I to withstand the power of the Almighty? He prevailed. And in that hour that I yielded not only my heart, but my *all* on the altar of love to be, to do, to go, as He chose—there was a great calm! There was peace, unspeakable peace, peace hitherto unknown! Now I could sing, "He took all my burden away."

The Lord works in a very gracious manner. On Sunday we had communion in our church. We sat quite near the front in the afternoon service, and this meant passing out of church by way of the side door. To do this we had to pass the platform. As I came to the steps of the platform, the minister came down, and laying his hand lightly on my shoulder he said, "And, sister, when will you sit with us at this table of the Lord?" The elders watched, the people nearby gazed a bit too, but the minister did not mind. He knew that here was a soul undergoing a terrific struggle! He felt that he was pastor, and had to tend the lambs of the fold! Did he read on my face that I had peace in my heart? He had just announced that a special preparation class for those who wished to confess the Lord publicly would begin that week. So he said to me, "Will you come this week to the class?" And I replied, "Yes, dominee."

A few months later, forty-five men and women walked down the aisle of that church following their pastor, prepared to make public confession of Jesus as their Savior. I was the youngest of that group. The church was crowded to its utmost capacity. It was a very impressive service. Some adults received the sacrament of baptism. The forty-five who were making confession stood up and sang,

> *Within His house, the house of prayer,
>   I dedicate myself to God;
> Let all His saints His grace declare
>   And join to sound His praise abroad.

whereupon the congregation responded:

> *Yea, in His place of holiness
> Lift up your hands the Lord to bless;
>   And unto you be given
> The joys that Zion doth afford,
> The richest blessing of the Lord
>   Who made the earth and heaven.

---

*These psalms were sung in Dutch as all our services were then conducted in the Holland language.

Just as they are. Do they need the gospel?
See page 88.

CHAPTER III

"There's surely somewhere a lowly place,
 In Earth's harvest-field so wide,
Where I may labour through life's short day
 For Jesus the Crucified.
So, trusting my all to Thy tender care,
 And knowing Thou lovest me,
I'll do Thy will with a heart sincere,
 I'll be what Thou would'st have me to be."

CHAPTER III

PREPARATION FOR SERVICE—I

It was a beautiful mid-September day when, after saying good-bye to all my people, for I was not to come home again until the Christmas holiday, I went over to Brooklyn, New York, to enter as student at the Union Missionary Training Institute.

Up to this time, as far as I can remember, I had never read a single book on foreign missions. Nor had I ever heard a foreign missionary address. The names of such countries as China, Japan, India and Africa were familiar to me only through the school geography. As to conditions, and the need of the gospel in these lands I was entirely ignorant. Hence I entered missionary school with the purpose of becoming a city missionary, or possibly I might go to the red Indians of our land. The Indian country was to me like the end of the world, so far as missionary activity was concerned. You will probably make the remark, "What gross ignorance!" And I would answer, "What an awakening!" Contrast the year 1913 with the year 1926. We then had no mission study classes; no young people who had gone to the foreign fields; very few missionary addresses; and consequently there was little inspiration and enthusiasm for the great cause of world-evangelization to be found in our particular denomination—the Christian Reformed Church. But today we have a foreign field of our own; more volunteers for missionary service than the church can place; and an ever-increasing zeal for this tremendous task, viz.: bringing the gospel of Jesus Christ to the uttermost bounds of this earth.

And though I was still young, I would not have you think that I was indifferent to the needs of the people about us.

On Saturday afternoons I would rush home from the office to

attend the gospel meeting in the county jail. At least two or three evenings a week I gave to attend meetings on the street corner, or in the tiny Mission Hall. And many other evangelistic meetings did I attend—all in connection with the work of the Star of Hope Mission, of Paterson, N. J. How true it was,

> "What a wonderful change in my life has been wrought,
>   Since Jesus came into my heart."

No longer could I be satisfied with the fellowship of those former friends; no longer was there any desire for the pleasures of this world. Christ had planted a new affection. The places I once loved, now I shunned. And the work of the church and mission, which formerly I ridiculed, now I attended with strict regularity and with intense delight.

And so the day came when I stepped out of the office into the Training Institute. Away from the buzz of elevators, telephones and typewriters to the quiet seclusion of a dormitory room and the uplifting atmosphere of continual fellowship with believers and intensive Bible study.

However, for three whole weeks I refused to unpack my trunk. "Fightings within and fears without" seemed to be my daily experience during those weeks. Then billows of doubt seemed to roll over my soul. "Shall I return home?" "Shall I give up believing that God would have my life for His service?" "Dare I ask to dream a dream or see a vision, or hear an angel voice to confirm God's will for me?" These were the attacks of the enemy, who took advantage of me at a time when, as never before, I was feeling my utter unworthiness to be a messenger of the King. How often have I noticed that Satan works in just this way. Jesus, immediately after His baptism, the open heaven, the Father's voice, the manifestation of the Spirit, was led into the wilderness to be tempted of the Devil. Just as soon as we take an advance step for our God, Satan will come with his attacks to drag us back or cause us to side-step. It is at such a time that we need to be specially prepared, remembering that

> "No man, having put his hand to the plough, and
>   looking back, is fit for the kingdom of God."

But after those first three weeks there came a settled peace, and the assurance that I was in the place where God would have me be.

For three years I was privileged to be at this Training Institute. We had a wonderful staff of teachers. Men and women—professors, ministers who had high degrees from universities in Europe, and medical doctors. They were all busy people, but they loved the Lord and His cause, and they freely gave one, two or three hours per week, to come and teach a group of young people who were going into missionary service. It would take pages to tell of them individually and thus I will refrain from mentioning any names. But just to illustrate. We had a certain dentist with a very large practice. He was offered a hundred dollars a lecture to give the same course at a big New York university that he was giving in our school. He had to refuse because he was too busy. And yet he came to us, one evening a week, teaching us *gratis* how to extract teeth, etc., etc. I shall never forget the introduction to his course, when he stood before us, and said, "Dear students, some of you will quite likely be going into the far-away places of the earth. You will be miles away from a doctor or dentist. I count it a great privilege to be able to give you a little help, and in days to come I shall think of you. Seeing I cannot go myself, this is the least I can do—help you to be more efficient in the great task before you. God bless you all!" And then he began a very helpful course of lectures on dentistry.

Bear with me for just one more illustration. A lady doctor sat before us. She had come twice a week to give us a course of lectures. She had gone abroad for continued study, and was a woman of very high reputation among those who practiced medicine. On this particular day she said, "Students, today I have come to a definite milestone in life. It is years since I first began the practice of medicine. Looking back, I rejoice to think of how many people I have been able to help, and with you all I would just now like to express my gratitude to God." She bowed her head, and offered a very earnest prayer of thanksgiving to Him, Who is the Giver of all good and perfect gifts.

Then we had missionaries come from all over the world and relate to us their experiences. They gave us advice and encouraged us on our way.

We also had practical mission work to do. We went to the slum districts on Saturday afternoon to do visitation work; on Sunday afternoon we taught in some Mission Sunday School, and some of us had special work. During my third year I went three times each month to a Prison-Rescue Home for girls, to hold a gospel service. These girls, having fallen by the wayside, were brought before a court judge, but were given a chance to learn and to prove their behavior. Thus they were sent to this Home to be there until they had reached the age of twenty-one. Some were as young as fourteen and fifteen when they entered. In reality they were prisoners. Every door and window was heavily barred and locked. But the girls had school classes, housework, sewing lessons, Sunday School, and these gospel meetings. I was always glad to go to these poor girls with a message from the Book. As I looked into their faces, I realized that, but for the grace of our God, I might have been among them.

This training was not at all easy. The class-work was heavy, demanding much study, and the examinations came with strict regularity. The building was old, and in winter we suffered much cold in the dormitory rooms. The school was poor and consequently the food was not all that could be desired. It may not be amiss to tell you just a little of this side.

The school year started in September, and I remember we went along until February, and we had never seen a whole egg on our plate. As students we would talk in our room about the meals. Then we would say to each other, "Prunes, prunes, always prunes!" We were thoroughly tired of prunes, and then began to joke about them, and call them "Missionary school strawberries." What a stretch of the imagination! To be eating prunes, and try to make yourself believe they taste like fresh strawberries.

And about once a week we had a wonderful pudding for dessert. The remains of the morning porridge, oatmeal, hominy, corn-meal, etc., etc., was all gathered together for some days.

and then an egg, some sugar and milk, and a few raisins added, baked in the oven, and served as pudding. To this pudding we gave a fancy name. We called it "Review of Reviews!"

The neighboring churches often had a social, a supper, or something of the sort. And whatever was left would be given to the missionary students. These surprise packages generally contained lovely sandwiches, rich cake, and sometimes some other rare dainties. But then again we would have our mouth all set for something nice and would get a real disappointment. How well I remember one day. It was Monday morning. A telephone message came to ask whether we could send two young men students to a church only a couple blocks away. The boys were hustled off to get back in time for the nine o'clock class. Very soon they returned, carrying a washboiler between them. What could that contain? The church had feasted on a turkey supper on Friday night, but the person who was to call up the school on Saturday, quite naturally forgot. So the remains of the turkey supper were found in the church basement on Monday morning, and our boys sent to collect them. What were these "remains"? To my utter horror, there was a washboiler half full of turkey bones! There was nothing else! Well, some of us thought we possessed just a little Christian grace, but we were truly angry on this particular morning. We asked the cook to throw them away, lest we get ptomaine poison. We came to the table at noon, to find that we were having soup that day. But with some of us, the anger had not abated and we said, "No, thank you" as the dishes of hot turkey-bone broth were passed around.

I have not exaggerated this story one little bit. It happened only once in the three years I was there that we were treated so shamefully. The old idea, "any person is good enough for the mission field," and "anything is good enough for missionaries and missionary students," was quite frequently emphasized at that time.

Let me not give you the idea, however, that we never had good things to eat. Some people and some churches treated us royally. I do not know the name of the man, but there was a very generous brother in that big neighborhood. This brother had a sister in China. She was a missionary. This brother also had a fish market. And every Saturday we had a delicious dinner of fresh fish—the gift of this Christian brother to the missionary students. Another regular gift was the annual Thanksgiving dinner, an elaborate affair, donated by one of the churches where some of our students attended.

True, it was wonderful training for young people preparing to go to the foreign field. We all had to do our own washing and ironing, as well as keep our own rooms clean. How we laughed one day when one of the boys—a Holland young man eager to keep up our reputation of cleanliness—boiled a pair of colored socks!

But this training proved too strenuous for some young people. Very hard study, poor dormitory accommodation, insufficient supply of certain necessary foodstuffs began to tell on some students. I know of at least five who went out from the walls of that Training Institute with tuberculosis during the three years I was there. And our student body never numbered over thirty at that time. Some of us had relatives who sent us parcel post packages. Some of us had a fair bit of spending money and could buy some things we liked. But others were poor. One young man, a classmate of mine, came over here from Denmark to continue his studies. He was an artist, and had a splendid education, having studied three years in Germany before coming to America. But he was poor! During vacation and holiday time he worked and painted pictures, so as to earn his tuition and money for clothes. One day he told me how he was sent to speak at a certain meeting, and only had carfare to get there. But after the meeting several men shook hands with him, and one placed in his hand a five-dollar bill. This was the Lord's abundant provision for the return carfare. At the graduation exercises he gave a paper on "The Sudan." His purpose was to continue his studies at some seminary for two years, and then go out to the Sudan, Africa. But God's purpose was otherwise. Within a half-year after graduation this young life was cut off. He died from hasting tuberculosis.

After three years of training in such an institution one should be able to say with the great Apostle Paul:

> "I have learned in whatsoever state I am,
> therewith to be content."

Lest you should think that such conditions still prevail, I must tell you that the school long since gave up these buildings. Today the Union Missionary School, of Brooklyn, is amalgamated with the National Bible Institute, of New York, and there is a fine, up-to-date, fireproof building, with a very much larger student enrollment. I rejoice with great joy at this marvelous advance— the token of God's care and grace!

Boarding school pupils exercising. See page 139.

CHAPTER IV

*"Go out into the highways and hedges
and compel them to come in, that
my house may be filled."*

LUKE 14:23

CHAPTER IV

PREPARATION FOR SERVICE—II

In the previous chapter I told you how I went over to Brooklyn, N. Y., to receive training at a Bible Institute there.

Three years had elapsed! How fast the time flies! It seemed like a dream on that morning when we packed our trunks after all the excitement of final examinations and graduation exercises. However, we all felt that we were one step nearer our goal. Now we had a diploma, and for each of us the day was near when we might begin actual missionary work. Some were to engage in service at home; others had their eyes fixed on South America; another felt a definite call to India; while China's millions appealed to one, "Come over and help *us.*" As we disbanded that morning, we were not unmindful of the fact that we might never again in this world see some of these familiar faces. And so it proved to be. Before the end of that year, as I mentioned in the previous chapter, we received the message of one fellow-student, who, instead of going into Africa's night of heathenism and superstition, was called to enter the Gloryland, the Land where darkness is unknown because there is no setting sun.

Many people were surprised to hear that I felt a special leading to go to Africa, should the Lord permit.

It was during the summer previous to my last year in school. I had been sent to represent the school at a large Missionary Conference at Lake Geneva, Wisconsin. Among the many speakers at this ten-day conference was Dr. H. K. W. Kumm, Ph.D., F. R. G. S. One evening he spoke for over an hour, telling of the conditions in the Sudan; vividly picturing before our minds the many tribes of Central Africa untouched by the gospel message, and in danger of being won over to the religion of the false prophet Mohammed. I sat spellbound! Not a word of this message escaped my attention! I was profoundly impressed and deeply moved! I went to my tent and retired, but sleep refused to still my thought! I spent three days in prayer and meditation.

Up to this time I felt no desire to enter upon foreign missionary service. But now there seemed to be a clear Macedonian call from over the sea. There were no friends near with whom I could talk the matter over. I wrestled with the Lord to know His will as to whether He was calling me into this special foreign missionary work. And on the third day I yielded my will to the Lord of the harvest, to obey Him even to some remote part of His harvest-field.

> "Have Thine own way, Lord,
> Have Thine own way!
> Hold o'er my being
> Absolute sway!"

During that last year in school I made special effort to get all the information I could on Africa. I was in personal touch with Dr. Kumm, at that time secretary for the American branch of the Sudan United Mission, with which I am now connected.

It was not possible to go from the missionary school direct to Africa. I was told that, due to climatic conditions over there, the Board could not sanction my going until I was twenty-five years old. That meant I was to be patient and wait three whole years.

Several offers for service here at home came to me just previous to graduation from the Training Institute.

In August of that year I came to Michigan to begin city mission work under the auspices of the Eastern Avenue Christian Reformed Church, of which Rev. J. Groen was at that time pastor.

The agreement was that I should work one year, and that I be allowed to take up the courses in Reformed Doctrine at our Calvin College. It would take several chapters to tell in detail of the work of that year. But the practical experience in mission work at home has been of tremendous help and value to me in working in Africa. For this reason I am devoting so much space to this important subject of "Preparation for Service."

Regular visitation work was done in a given district; a store was rented and Mission Sunday School was begun. Later a class for boys and a sewing class for girls was also started. Each week I had a gospel meeting in two factories. I went at least once a month to the Tuberculosis Sanatorium and did personal work with the patients. I had a class for training in personal work in the church; and a short course for those who were teaching in the Mission Sunday School.

As to the results of this work I would rather we wait until that Great Day when the Judge of all the earth will speak.

At Calvin College they had a Student Volunteer Band, organized several years before, of which I was the first woman member. The members of this band were desirous that our church people should become acquainted with the conditions and needs of the different foreign mission fields. I was asked by them to go on a deputation tour for this purpose. "Who is to be responsible for the expenses?" I asked. And they replied, "We have never had dues or collections at the band meetings, and hence we have no treasury." Thinking the matter over, I said, "I have not been able to save any money this year." (My salary was far less than what I had earned as stenographer when only fifteen years old.) "But I have five dollars, and that will take me somewhere. So I am willing to start out."

Being convinced that the time had come for a man to take over the work of the mission, and desiring to continue some further study in the near future, I left the mission work in Grand Rapids, and went to Northern Michigan, where I had several appointments to speak and present the needs of the different foreign mission fields. At each place I was given $5.00, and proceeded to Chicago to do the same there. On and on, for four months, I went traveling about, entering every open door and setting forth the cry of the heathen world. At the end of this trip I had $150.00 balance, which was put in the bank, and later applied to my expenses in going to Africa. In a wonderful way, the Lord taught me that if we put our trust in Him, we small never be put to shame. This experience also greatly stimulated my faith.

Again I turned my face to the great world city—New York, to continue training. This time I entered a Special Maternity Hospital, and after a year of very strenuous effort, received a diploma, plus a government certificate to practice midwifery. The Mission Board, under which I already had a definite appointment to go to Africa, recommended to me to take up such a course. In subsequent chapters I may have occasion to explain what a blessing it has been to me in Africa, where medical help is so very scarce.

It seemed now that I might soon set sail for the far away heathen field. But here I am reminded of a mission secretary who was interviewing a candidate with a view to an appointment for service. Said the aged secretary to the young man who was applying: "Dear young brother, there are three definite requirements for a missionary candidate. I would like to impress that fact upon you. The first thing you need is PATIENCE; don't forget that. The second thing you need is more important than the first, it is PATIENCE; and the third is so important that if you do not have it, you will be an utter failure—it is P A T I E N C E!"

How hard it is, when we are conscious of a great need, and have a burning passion to go out and "tell the gospel story," to wait and wait and wait! What boundless patience it does require, lest we should murmur or doubt our high calling.

For six or eight months I was again engaged in City Mission work, this time with the Hebrew Mission of Paterson, N. J.

At last, permit received, passport duly signed, passage reservation engaged, a definite date was set when I was to sail from New York to Africa.

A minister once made this wise statement: "An ocean journey will not make a missionary out of anyone. Another minister once said: "A soul at home is of equal value to a soul abroad!" And a third man of God said: "If you have no concern for the salvation of men and women at home, you will never have a passion for the lost world outside." And to all this I wholeheartedly say "Amen."

There are too many Christian workers who have lifted their gaze to the shores of some distant land, and who are utterly indifferent to the needs of the people in their own community.

At the Fifth Avenue Presbyterian Church in New York, I heard Dr. Jowett say: "Every Christian should have a daily period of communion with God. One should engage in Bible reading and prayer, as well as quiet meditation. As a part of that meditation it is well at times to think back—to reflect—upon all the way in which God has led you."

Today as I reflect—as I review a little of the past, I remember that in several prisons; in rescue homes; in hospitals and sanatoriums; in saloons, in dens of vice, on New York's Great White Way and in her Chinatown; in a gypsy camp; in alms houses; on the street corners of several cities; in different mission halls; in numerous private homes; to a few rich; to many of the poor of the poorest—have I been privileged to testify to the "depth of the riches of love in Christ Jesus."

And in my humble opinion, this is a most valuable part of a missionary's preparation for service in the foreign field.

Tapping wine from the palm tree. See page 105.

CHAPTER V

"Be strong and of a good courage; be not afraid, neither be thou dismayed for the Lord thy God is with thee whithersoever thou goest."

CHAPTER V

"IN JOURNEYINGS OFTEN . . ."

We will now again pick up the thread which was broken at the end of the first chapter.

The great Mauretania moved along slowly and quietly on her way to England, passing New York's skyscraper buildings, and giving us a last look at the Statue of Liberty. Remembering the historic significance of this massive statue, and realizing that we were sailing away from the shores of our beloved homeland, one could hardly help breathe the prayer:

> Protect us by Thy might,
> Great God, our King!

Very soon we were out into the great Atlantic. Speed was increased! Land was left far behind! All one could see was water and sky.

I went down to my cabin, and found it rather crowded. It was the year after the Armistice, and one could not pick and choose how one wished to travel. This was an inside cabin, and there were two other women and two children besides myself. What a time we had getting our baggage in order! The mother and two children were Austrians, and they were going over to the old country to greet their family that was suffering grief and loss, due to the war. The other lady was Scotch, and was also traveling for the same purpose.

The first three days all went well. Everybody was cheerful because the sea was calm and one could enjoy the fresh ocean air. But then we ran into a very heavy storm. The waves rose like black, snowcapped mountains, and dashed against the vessel! The big ship began to roll and toss! One after another the passengers left the deck to go to their cabins. And for three whole

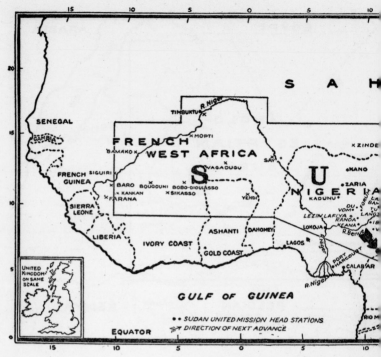

Map showing mission stations in the Sudan.

days this storm raged! The wind blew with such violence that it tore loose a heavy staircase on the upper deck. A lifeboat was also thrown into the great deep. Though there were hundreds of passengers, there was one day, when the storm was furious, that not a single woman could go to the dining room.

What a long three days! What a dreadful thing it is to be so terribly seasick! Who cares what happens to the trunks as they bang to and fro against one another? Who thinks about a meal when they hear an awful noise and learn that stacks of dishes were thrown to the floor and broken?

Fear led many people to cry unto the Lord to deliver them from the dangers of the deep.

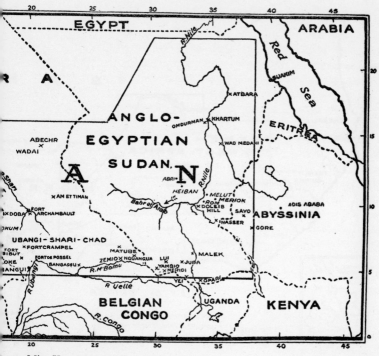

ts to Miss Veenstra's station. See page 71.

At last the wind began to calm down; the sun smiled upon us from the heaven above; the roaring of the waves gradually grew fainter, and the vessel moved more steadily. One after another the passengers again sought the fresh air. Many looked pale and exhausted, but each bore a cheerful expression of hope and gratitude while exchanging a hearty word of greeting.

Due to this storm we were delayed in getting to our port. It was not an effort to stay up until midnight to see the lights of the shore line. There was much excitement as we anchored, but we were told that no one would be permitted to leave the ship until morning, and so we retired.

Everybody was up on time the next morning. Several officers

boarded the ship to examine our papers. Such a host of questions, and such endless red tape. How thankful I was when the man said to me: "Your papers are complete—pass on."

There was a special train to take passengers to London. So I walked over to the ticket office, after having my trunks examined by the custom officers, and asked for a ticket to London.

"What class?" promptly enquired the ticket agent.

"Third class, please," replied the missionary.

The English trains are a little different to our American ones. The coaches are divided into separate compartments. Each compartment is large enough to accommodate six or eight passengers. The passengers travel first, second or third class, according to their social standing and according to their pocketbook. Most missionaries and ministers travel third class, as well as the greatest majority of the traveling public. It is every bit as comfortable as our American day coaches.

This was my first glimpse of England. The scenery was beautiful. Small farms, neat hedges, brooks and streams with pretty little bridges, thatched farmhouses, were to be seen all along the way.

After three hours the train slowed down and we came to that crowded, wonderful, old city of London.

Someone has written a book bearing the title "Alone in London." That was my experience just now. There was no one to meet me, as I failed to send a telegram message to the mission office. The few porters at the station devoted all their attention to the first class passengers. So we hauled about our own luggage, dragging the trunks from the baggage car to some central spot until we had all our belongings together. It was the year after the war, and everything was much upset in England. Traveling was very hard. It was also next to impossible to get accommodation. I asked the taxi driver to take me to the Y. W. C. A. (In England this institution provides sleeping accommodation for women.) He said, "Why, Madam, every Y. W. C. A. place is overcrowded. If you have not made reservation, it will be useless to go." I then asked him, "What about the hotels?" "You'll never get in a hotel," he said, "they have long waiting lists."

Then I gave him the address of our mission office in London, and asked him to take me there.

Like a thunderbolt out of a clear sky I walked into the office of the mission and introduced myself. They were surprised, and also perplexed. The secretary had written to America to say that I was not to come just yet, as he could not get passage booked for me from England to West Africa. This letter, however, arrived in America after I had set sail.

Well, the first thing to do was to get my four pieces of baggage from the taxi into the office and pay the driver, so he could be excused. This done, I sat down, and the secretary, Mr. Dawson, very kindly said to me, "I will again 'phone the steamship company about a passage for West Africa." The result of that 'phone call was: "The company says they are not able to give us a reservation for you until the middle or end of February."

"Does that mean that I shall have to wait here in England from today, October 10th, to the middle or end of February, next year?" I enquired.

"Yes, and what is more," said Mr. Dawson, "It is so difficult to get sleeping accommodations. We are living two families in one small house. The little baby sleeps in the bureau drawer at night. Everybody is crowded, and all the hotels likewise."

This was just about all I could stand. It was nearly midafternoon. I had had nothing to eat since early morning. The day was cold and damp. The big city was so strange, and among its thousands of people there was not one I knew. One of my trunks had slipped and fallen on my foot, and this was painful. And now this disheartening word about further passage just made me wish I was back in the U. S. A. I started to cry, though I tried so hard to keep the tears back.

Then they asked me whether I had had lunch. And I replied "No."

So I was taken to a nearby restaurant and had a cup of hot cocoa, and a little lunch, and this helped to take away a good bit of the gloom.

One of the missionaries, being home on furlough, just then in the office, went out to search for a place for me.

In the evening he took me to a very kind Christian woman, an American, who had a large home for missionaries traveling to and fro, and she so lovingly greeted and welcomed me. At once a heavy load seemed to be lifted, and the world seemed quite normal again.

Then I began to pray and ask the Lord to open the way so that I might not have to wait all this time in England. After a few days, I believed that my prayer would be answered, and that by the end of the year I would be started on my next ocean journey for the west coast of Africa. The secretary, Mr. Dawson, did not encourage me in this. He said, "It will only be possible if someone else cancels their passage, and seeing there are so very few women traveling to West Africa, makes it even more difficult."

October and November went by. December came, and everybody was making plans for Christmas. The year would soon be ended, and there seemed not the slightest intimation that I might get a passage.

One day, the 22nd, I came in at noon, and there was a telegram message for me. How eagerly I tore open that message and read and re-read the following, "Passage booked for you December 31st."

This incident tremendously strengthened my faith. Only nine days did I have to get ready, for I had still my tropical outfit to buy. But what a joy it was to know that now I would be on the ocean, en route to West Africa, and would not hear the "Old Year ring out and the New Year ring in." We had special prayer of thanksgiving, and sang,

> "All the way my Savior leads me,
> What have I to ask beside?"

* * * * * * * *

The steamer from Liverpool to Lagos was very small compared with the Mauretania. Most of the passengers were men, government officials, traders, miners, and some who had other positions in the larger towns along the coast. There were only nine women passengers. There were four missionaries aboard.

Once again we were thrown into "perils in the sea." You may remember that in January, 1920, a large steamer—I believe a French boat—was thrown upon the rocks just off the coast of Spain. Over three hundred people went down into the deep and perished. We were on the ocean in this same storm. For two days the captain was not able to turn the boat, and we were heading straight for New York. I remember one night that we could not sleep at all, due to the excessive motion of the ship. We had to hold ourselves down into the berth. On the fourth day the storm ceased, but the water was still very rough. On the sixth day I left the cabin for the first time since boarding the vessel. It is marvelous how the fresh air revives and stimulates one. And the trip became a real pleasure when we once entered the tropical waters. In a few days we came out of the bitter cold in midwinter to the burning sun of the tropics. It was also very interesting to stop at different ports along the West African coast.

On the nineteenth day all four missionaries disembarked at Lagos. Two of the missionaries had their home and work right there in this large town. It being Sunday, they took me along to their home. The next morning I was to get a train to go up country.

Here at Lagos was evidence that the "Gospel of Jesus Christ is the power of God unto salvation." In the evening I was taken into a beautiful large church, and heard a splendid sermon. The message was in English and given by a native minister. Today this man, an African, is promoted to the high position of Bishop. For over a hundred years the Church Missionary Society of England has been working at several coast towns. And today they have a large ordained native ministry, many trained evangelists, thousands of converts, large church buildings, and several schools of high standing.

Early Monday morning the train pulled out of Lagos. I was to go as far as Minna, making a journey of from twenty-four to thirty hours in the train. A telegram had been sent to the missionaries at Minna asking them to meet me at the station, as I was traveling alone.

The barge in which the author spent 14 days with a native crew on her first journey inland. See page 64.

Arriving there, I found a splendid station, with school, chapel, and printing establishment. But the missionaries were in sorrow. The day before I arrived they had received a message of the death of one of their single lady missionaries, at some remote station. The girl who died was a Canadian, and out on her first term of service. She walked out early one morning and was bitten by a very small, deadly poisonous black snake. On the third day, after violent convulsions, just before the doctor arrived, she passed away. Of course this news was a great shock to all the other workers.

For three days I was at this station, and then continued my journey by taking another train from Minna to Baro, traveling from morning until evening.

At this place there was no mission station, and I had to wait five days for the arrival of a small steamer to take me to Lokoja. There was a trading center here, with a few white men in charge. They were very kind to me and helpful, and I had a splendid opportunity to speak to them about their need of the Lord and His saving grace.

The next journey was pleasant. I boarded a very small steamer and we sailed over the broad Niger River from dawn until seven o'clock in the evening, when we anchored at Lokoja, where a missionary was waiting to meet me.

There are so few white people in the interior of Africa, that it is not hard to make acquaintance. And one readily feels at home with missionaries.

So, after a good clean-up, we had our evening meal, and sat outside to enjoy a beautiful evening in the tropics. This missionary had been in the country for years, and belonged to the Church Missionary Society of England. We chatted quite a while, and it seemed I answered no end of questions, when he said: "Now I will tell you the situation. You still have the river journey to make. As far as we know there are no other missionaries coming soon, and due to the extreme heat at this place, I should judge it unwise for you to remain here any longer than necessary. Would you be afraid to make that journey alone?"

"How many days would it take me?" I asked.

"All of two weeks," he answered.

"Do you think it would be all right for me to go on alone?"

"As far as I know no white woman has ever taken that journey alone. You are at a disadvantage by being new, unaccustomed to the country, the climate and the people. And you do not have the language. But, seeing you have come this far alone, I think it would be all right. However I shall have to speak to the government official in the morning and ask him."

The next morning I was introduced to the government official. He asked me several questions, especially regarding what training I had received in medical work. From Lokoja to Ibi was almost three hundred miles, and there was no doctor in all that distance. For this reason the official wanted to find out whether I would know what to do in case I became ill on the way. After a little he agreed with the missionary that I should proceed, and at once we began to make arrangements.

A river barge was hired from one of the trading places. This barge was a flat-bottom steel boat. It was divided into four sections, having a small roof over the two center sections which was to be my home for two weeks. It was all open, without a cabin and dressing room. My baggage was to be in the third section, while the fourth would act as a kitchen, where my food and the food of the natives would be cooked.

Next in order, a crew had to be found. This only took an hour. A reliable headman with twelve other men who were to do the poling, a youth to act as cook for the entire crew, and the wife of the headman, a company of fourteen Africans who were to accompany me. Besides this was a lad who was to do my cooking and marketing.

With the help of the kind missionary a supply of foodstuffs was bought at the market, and deposited in the barge. Sweet potatoes, yams, eggs, onions, peanut butter oil for frying, etc., etc., plus a couple of small live West African fowls.

By late afternoon we were all ready. The missionary took me down to the river beach, giving me some final instructions and advice, especially urging me to drink no water unless it was thoroughly boiled. He gave some further instructions to the headman and the crew, but I did not understand a word of this, as it was in the Hausa language. We shook hands, he left the barge, and the polers pushed hard and soon the little boat was started on its long journey up the Binue River.

About sundown the crew began to argue. I could not say a word, as I did not understand what it was all about. Later I could reason it out. Some wanted to stop and anchor for the night at a certain nearby sandbank. Others wanted to push on some more before they stopped for the night. I saw one pull out from his leather girdle a native knife, a long pointed instrument, over an inch wide. This looked to me for all the world like a dagger, and I began to be afraid. Would they dare to kill me, and throw my body into the river, and steal my baggage?

At last we stopped. The men jumped from the barge to the sandbank, fastened the boat, unrolled their sleeping mats, made a little fire, and sat around to palaver. Then, seated around two large bowls of food, they enjoyed their evening meal. After this they went to sleep. I stayed in the barge, and just managed to get my camp bed put up in the largest section. But this experience was all so new for me. And I was still not sure about the use of that knife. So for a long while I tossed and tossed, finally dropping off to sleep.

Early in the morning we pushed off again. With the fresh strength the men were able to push hard and the poles swayed with perfect rhythm. We went quite fast until about nine o'clock, when we stopped so the crew could have breakfast. I got out and walked around the sandbank for some exercise.

Though I could not talk with anyone, seeing they understood no English, the days did not seem to drag. I had a good bit of reading material, and many letters to write, as well as some sewing, and would rest to enjoy the scenery along the river bank. One day the men called out to me, and then pointed in a certain direction. Sure enough, there was a lion, right at the edge of the river. He had come for a drink. This was the first wild animal I saw in Africa, and it gave me quite a thrill.

On the sixth day I was not able to rise in the morning. Every

"First fruits" of the gospel. Taken in front of the chapel-school hut. See page 175.

time I lifted my head I got so dizzy and faint, and would have to lie down again. I did not know what this strange feeling could mean. Toward noon it was some better, and I got up. In the evening we came to a rather large town, and stopped for the night. There was a white man here who had charge of a trading center. Hearing of our arrival, he came down to see me, and invited me up to his house for the evening meal. I accepted, and told him of the strange dizziness in my head that morning. He was able to diagnose it at once. He said it was due to the reflection of the sun on the water, that I should be very careful, wear my helmet, etc., as it was a very bad thing to get an attack of sun in Africa.

For the rest of the journey all went well. On the fifteenth day after leaving Lokoja, we arrived at Ibi, and here I was met by the field secretary of the Sudan United Mission. Now I felt at home. After our greeting, he said to me, "It has been decided that you are to go to the Takum district where we are about to open a new station." Then he smiled and added, "They are a cannibal people, but I hope you won't be eaten. However, you won't be going just immediately. You can go up to the house, and I will see to your baggage."

At four o'clock we had tea. After that Mr. F—— asked me, "Do American ladies ride a bicycle?" I replied, "Not like they do in England, but many of our girls ride." "What about yourself, have you ever been on a wheel?" "Yes, when a girl, but that is many years ago." "Fine, one never forgets. We will go and try."

There was a lady's wheel that I could use pro tem, and out to the path we strolled. I managed a mile or two, and he said that would do. "In the morning you will go to Wukari. Mr. H—— will accompany you."

"How far is Wukari from here, please?" I asked.

"About twenty-five miles."

"Can we make that in one day on the bicycle?"

"I think you'll manage it all right."

The next morning Mr. H—— and I were off at dawn. I pushed and pushed, but that was a long twenty-five miles. We sat on the roadside and had a sandwich and a drink of water.

Then we pushed some more. The sun grew so hot. Not accustomed to this heat, my heart began to beat so fast. Every hill we came to, I would get off and walk. Then at last, about eleven o'clock, we came to Wukari, and there I drank about seven cups of hot tea.

After another week I was to go on to Donga, another twenty-five miles, where I would be stationed for some months for language study, etc.

Before graduating from missionary school, I had chosen as a life motto a certain verse from Joshua. All along this journey, from New York to the great Sudan in Central Africa, I was strengthened by this life-motto text:

> "Be strong and of good courage; be not
> afraid, neither be thou dismayed: for
> the Lord thy God is with thee whither-
> soever thou goest."

Boarding school pupils in school dress. See page 139.

CHAPTER VI

The fields are white unto the harvest, Lord,
  Their golden treasures wait on every side;
But how shall all their priceless wealth be stored?
  The reapers are so few—the world so wide.
    Lord, send the labourers forth!

The fields are Thine, with Love's great ransom bought,
  The precious blood of Thy beloved Son;
'Tis long since His redeeming work was wrought,
  Yet scarce the reaping seems to be begun.
    Lord, send the labourers forth!

To us, Thy people, whom Thou hast redeemed,
  To us belong the sin, the humbling shame;
We have not reaped, we have but slept and dreamed,
  Nor called with holy ardour on Thy name.
    Lord, send the labourers forth!

Awake Thy Church, ere yet the day departs,
  For while she sleeps swift works the reaper, Death;
O God, forgive, and into torpid hearts
  Send, like a mighty wind, Thy quickening breath!
    Lord, send the labourers forth!

Come from the South, O Wind! come from the North,
  And from thy garden make the spices flow!
Their fragrance sweet throughout the earth shed forth,
  Till God's great gift to men all men shall know.
    Lord, send the labourers forth!

The glory, Father, shall be Thine; Thy Son
  With joy the fruit of all His travail see;
Thy will on earth shall as in heaven be done,
  And heaven and earth make one full harmony.
    Lord, send the labourers forth!

CHAPTER VI

THE CALL OF THE SUDAN

*The Sudan is that part of Africa lying immediately south of the Sahara and Egypt, stretching from the Gambia and Senegal in the west to Abyssinia in the east, and having for its southern boundaries, Liberia, Ivory Coast, Gold Coast, Dahomey, Southern Nigeria, Southern Cameroons, Belgian Congo and Uganda. It is not an exactly defined geographical entity, but this description of its limits is generally accepted. Its name is said to be part of a term applied to it by the Arabs and others from North Africa, who, crossing the Great Desert, came to a country where the people were mainly of a darker colour than themselves, and named it Bilad-es-Sudan, "The Land of the Blacks."

This vast region is now under the control of Great Britain and France, but *until twenty-five years ago the greater part of it was largely closed to Europeans.* As a result of this, it was only when the power of the slave-raiding Moslem emirates had been broken, and their victims and enemies, the pagan tribes, warring also amongst themselves, had been brought under administration by the British and French governments, that the country became open to missionary effort; although previous attempts had been made and lives laid down to enter and claim the Sudan for Christ. When taken over by the European governments, great sections of the country had been devastated and millions of the people slaughtered, largely in the previous half-century, by the constant slave-raiding and inter-tribal warfare. The evangelization of the Sudan is therefore a thing of comparatively recent origin and growth, all missionary effort, save at a few centers, having been begun within the past twenty years, and much of it during the last decade.

The Sudan is occupied by hundreds of tribes of people, most of them speaking different languages, or dialects of the same language so varied as almost to constitute a different tongue. Roughly speaking, the peoples of the northern section of the region are Mohammedan in faith, while in the southern portion the tribes are pagan; but there are Mohammedan towns and colonies here and there among the pagans, and pagan tribes may still be found in the Moslem areas. The varied stages of civilization reached by these peoples cover a wide range, from the comparatively advanced social organization of the powerful Mohammedan emirates, with their written laws, history and literature, to the loose structure of the primitive and wild cannibal tribes, divided into quarreling clans and families, uniting only to meet a common foe.

In 1904, the Sudan United Mission was organized to evangelize the Sudan because at the time no other society could undertake to meet this urgent need. Largely owing to the propaganda of the mission, other societies are now helping to occupy the field, but nowhere does the S. U. M. encroach upon their work. Its missionaries are engaged in pioneer work on virgin soil, taking the gospel of Salvation to peoples who had no chance of receiving it otherwise, and who are now hearing for the first time the message which has been known to us and to our fathers for so many generations.

The Sudan United Mission has already begun work among some thirty tribes in Nigeria, Western Sudan, French Central Sudan, Anglo-Egyptian Sudan on the eastern side of the continent.

There are many tribes of people in the Sudan still waiting for the messengers of the Lord Jesus Christ. One could travel 1,500 miles through Central Sudan, visiting tribe after tribe, each with its different customs and languages, and in all that distance there would be found only a few missionaries of the gospel. Going in another direction, through the Western Sudan, a thousand miles could be traversed in which only about a score of witnesses for Christ would be discovered.

Mohammedan missionaries are to be met with in large and increasing numbers. Traders from the Mohammedan tribes are penetrating into the pagan districts in all directions, and every one of them, true to his faith, acts as a missionary for the false prophet. Following the traders are the teachers, who set up schools to teach the Koran, capturing the young people.

If the gospel is not speedily taken to the many pagan peoples of the Sudan, the next generation will be Mohammedan.

Now they are open and ready to listen to the gospel of the Lord Jesus Christ; *then* they will be antagonistic to Him as Lord and Savior, they will deny His deity, His atonement, and His resurrection; for Mohammedanism is a strongly anti-Christian faith. *Now,* as pagans, they welcome the gospel as a message of salvation from the bondage of their fetishism; *then,* as Mohammedans, they will reject the gospel with scorn and unbelief.

"For five years I have been watching the road for the coming of a teacher." So said a chief in the Sudan to one of the Sudan United Mission workers. As yet we have not been able to send a teacher to him and his people.

He still waits! ! !

And the Savior also waits! ! !

To whom shall they go—CHRIST or MOHAMMED?

------

*Most of this chapter I gathered from the very recent literature of the Sudan United Mission, with which I am connected.
                                                                    J. V.

Group of Lupwe boarding school pupils. See page 139.

CHAPTER VII

"Ask what I shall give thee . . .

"Give therefore thy servant an understanding heart . . ."

CHAPTER VII

GETTING ACQUAINTED

In the western part of the Sudan is found that large British protectorate, Nigeria. It is four times the size of Great Britain, and is, next to the Nile delta, the most densely populated region in Africa. Nigeria is divided politically into northern and southern provinces, with a combined population of eighteen and a half millions.

The Sudan United Mission is working in the northern province, which has a population of ten and a half millions. According to the last census it was found that there are over two hundred and fifty tribes, mostly speaking different languages.

Prior to 1901 there was only one mission station in the whole of Northern Nigeria, under the Church Missionary Society of England. The name of the station is Lokoja.

If you will turn to the map showing the mission stations in Northern Nigeria at the present day, you will note the tremendous advance during the past quarter of a century. You will note that twenty of these mission stations belong to the Sudan United Mission.

On the River Binue (No. 34), you will find a place called Ibi. This is the headquarters of our mission, and the place where I landed after the long river journey up the Binue from Lokoja. Twenty-five miles south of Ibi is Wukari (No. 35). This was my first bicycle trip in the Sudan. After a week at Wukari I proceeded to Donga, twenty-five miles southeast (No. 36). I was at Donga for seven months and then returned again to Wukari.

Everything was so new and strange. First there were the missionaries to meet and get acquainted with. Then, too, the country which was all so wild looking. No paved streets or straight paths. Just foot-trails. Not a single light at night, except it be moonlight. The missionaries had kerosene lamps. There were certain strict rules which had to be adhered to. Among them the following:

    a. Do not drink water that has not been thoroughly boiled.
    b. Never walk about in the dark without having on mosquito boots. (This is a high leather boot, and is also for protection against scorpions, centipedes, and snakes.)
    c. Take five grains of quinine daily to fight the fever.
    d. Do not risk going out in the sun without a helmet. (This is a broad-brim cork or rubber hat. It is heavy and awkward, and rather a burden at first, but a most wonderful invention for protection against the terrific rays of the sun.)

I shall not forget my second bicycle trip in Africa. It was one of those long twenty-five-mile rides. We started very early in the morning. In fact, as soon as we could see the outline of a path, we mounted the wheel. This was done to get the benefit of the cool of the morning. At first I was very nervous. A doctor was with me, and he said I was to ride first so as to set the pace and also so that, in case I should fall, he would be near. It was still dusk, and I prayed constantly to be able to *see the path*. After we got out five miles, the sun began to rise, and one had no difficulty in seeing the way. But now the path became more rugged, and in places very narrow with a kind of ditch on either side, and I found myself sighing, "O Lord, help me to *keep on the path*." About ten o'clock we saw in the bush a herd of very large deer with great long horns. Such beautiful creatures! The doctor, having a rifle with him, suggested we stop and he would try to shoot one. Leaving our wheels at a tree, we began to step softly into the bush so as to get nearer the deer. He fired a few shots, and struck one of them. But it was not a fatal shot, and hence he felt duty bound to trace the blood of the deer and try to shoot at him again. It would be unkind to leave a wounded animal to suffer. Well, this hunting expedition took over an hour of our time. Meanwhile the sun grew hotter, and we still had several miles to push the pedals. Just coming from a cold climate, I felt the heat very much. And not being used to the wheel as yet, my whole body seemed weak and sore. It was after lunch when we came to our destination, and I threw myself down to rest, wondering how many more days like this I might have in Africa.

The first duty of every missionary is to get a working knowledge of the language. It is impossible to get friendly with the people unless one can speak their tongue.

So, during the first year, the bulk of the time was spent at this tremendous task.

What terrific havoc the tower of Babel has wrought in this world! Every tribe we come to speaks a different tongue. And some of the pagan languages are so limited. No word for "sin," "repentance," "preach," "Holy Spirit," etc., etc., in many of these tongues. Think of what that means to the missionary.

Then one begins to do some school work. One wishes to teach the multiplication tables. For "twenty" these people in Donga say "one man"; for "forty" they say "two men." A man has ten fingers and ten toes—hence "twenty means one man."

4 times 5 equals one man

6 times 5 equals one man and ten (not one man and a half)

8 times 5 equals two men

Fifty miles from Donga you come to the tribe where I am at present. There the people speak an entirely different language. It is full of nasal sounds, plus a great many queer sounds which one can only make by exploding the breath from different parts of the mouth. Their system of numerals seems to go only as high as 5, and then begins over. As for example, to say 7, you must say "5 and 2." Think of teaching the multiplication tables in this tongue: 5 and 2 times 5 and 3 (meaning 7x8).

Many of these languages have not as yet been reduced to writing. It often takes years to get a single gospel translated into one of these tribal languages.

Most of our missionaries begin by learning the Hausa language. This is the trade language of Northern Nigeria, and used by the

Mohammedans. Their teachers are able to read and write the "character" form. The missionaries have translated (using the Roman letters) the entire New Testament, five books of the Old Testament, as well as several primers and books for school use.

By the end of this first year I had a working knowledge of this Hausa language, and was able to begin a little direct missionary work.

During the first year I treated many patients in the dispensary, and did some visiting among the people in company with some more experienced worker. There was ample opportunity to attend services in the chapel and to personally become acquainted with the converts and the people in general.

One day I had the joy of seeing a Christian couple (both converts of Wukari) united in marriage in the chapel. It was a Christian ceremony, the vows taken being the same as in our homeland. What an uplift and encouragement to a new worker to thus see the power of the gospel.

But this wedding day was also a funeral day. We passed from the ceremony of joy in the Christian chapel to the tiny cemetery half a mile away.

A certain young man, coming from some town a long way off, was taken ill at this place. He came to the dispensary, and the doctor (at that time we had a doctor at Wukari) sought to help him. It was proved he had cancer, and after quite a period of care and treatment, he died. While the doctor saw to the digging of the grave, another missionary and I wrapped the corpse for burial. I secretly hoped that I would not have much of this kind of work to do. We then wrapped the body in a grass mat, and after the wedding ceremony, the Christian young men carried it up to the place of burial. There the missionary spoke a few fitting words on the text, "I was a stranger, and ye took me in."

At the end of my first year, it was decided that I go along with another missionary, Rev. C. L. Whitman, who had already spent years in the country, where we were to open the new station in the Takum district among a cannibal people.

CHAPTER VIII

A cry, as of pain,
Again and again,
Is borne o'er the deserts and wide-spreading main;
A cry from the lands that in darkness are lying,
A cry from the hearts that in sorrow are sighing;
It comes unto me;
It comes unto thee;
Oh what—oh what shall the answer be?

CHAPTER VIII

ENTERING THE CANNIBAL DISTRICT

It was the first day of February, 1921, when we came to Lupwe, which was henceforth to be my permanent home. It was not a cold winter day, such as you may imagine, for we never have any winter in this part of Africa. February is about the hottest month of the year, and on this particular day, covering thirty miles on the wheel, we got a good share of sunburn.

For the Christmas holidays I had gone over to Donga, where we have a little group of Christians. After the festive season I settled down to pack all my belongings. There were a great many loads, each one weighing not more than sixty pounds, and when ready, I tried to find men who would take these loads and carry them (on their heads) to Lupwe, a distance of fifty-five miles. It was a great relief to see the last load carried out of the mission compound. For a week I had been at Donga alone, and now that all my possessions had gone on, I could start off the next morning. I was to go to Wukari, where another missionary would join me to continue part of the next journey. From Donga to Wukari is twenty-five miles, and for the major part of the way one meets very few people on the path.

Several of the Christians were at the mission compound early in the morning and came along with me to the bank of the river. Bidding them good-bye, I stepped into a small native canoe, together with three of the Christians who would see me over the river and safely across a large swamp on the other side of the river.

Nearly an hour had passed since we left the compound, and the morning time being so precious, I did not stop to talk much with anyone along the way, but hastily expressed my thanks and

[83]

appreciation to the Christians for their kindness and mounted the wheel. After pushing along about three miles, the front tire suddenly went flat. I stopped to see if the little leather case contained any material for mending a puncture. It did have a fair amount of patches, but no solution. So I was quite helpless. Hoping that it might not be a puncture, I unfastened the pump and began to pump up the tire. Then I mounted again, and rode about forty yards when all the air had escaped and it was as flat as before. I stood for a little while deliberating what to do. "Shall I go back?" This would be useless as I had sent off all my loads and provisions. "Shall I proceed to walk it?" Twenty-two miles is a long way to walk. I had only one water bottle, which would surely not suffice for a whole day. The bicycle not being my own I did not dare to ride it with a flat tire.

Then in my distress I cried unto the Lord, and asked Him to help me!

> What a friend we have in Jesus,
> All our cares and griefs to bear;
> What a privilege to carry
> Everything to God in prayer.

Once again I pumped up the tire and began to ride. Mile after mile, winding in and out, crossing small native-made bridges, noticing along the way here and there the fresh tracks of deer and antelope, listening to the familiar sound of the cricket, as well as the buzzing of other insects, I rode on. How sweetly the birds sang that morning! Nor was there any fear of wild animals! What was it that suddenly caused my spirit to be so glad?

> Heaven above is softer blue,
> Earth around is sweeter green!
> Something lives in every hue
> Christless eyes have never seen:
> Birds with gladder songs o'erflow,
> Flowers with deeper beauties shine,
> Since I know, as *now* I know,
> I am His and He is mine.

For eight miles I went along pushing, praying, singing, and watching the front tire. Looking up, I saw another bicycle approaching. It was one of the Wukari converts who had been taught to ride the wheel so that he might act as messenger in case of any emergency. The missionaries, knowing I was coming that morning, and thinking what a long lonely trail this was, very kindly sent this messenger to meet me and accompany me the rest of the journey. After the usual greeting, I told him the experience I had had with the tire, and we went on. When still about eight miles from Wukari, my front tire again went flat. The Christian youth said, "White lady, I will change the tires. I will give you one of mine, and then I will walk in the rest of the way." Out of the bush came a rather aged black man—a hunter. He had been out with spear, bow and arrows to see if he could find any meat. He stopped to greet us, and asked whether we were in trouble. Then L——, the young man who was with me said, "Yes, we have a little trouble, not much. We need rubber, but have none with us." The old hunter smiled, and said, "There is a rubber tree just off the path, will that not help you?" Looking up, L—— saw the rubber tree, went over to it, broke off a small branch, and there flowed a tiny bit of rubber. With this he was able to put on a patch, and thus repair the puncture.

How marvelous! In that part of the bush there are not many rubber trees. In His own wonderful way the Lord undertook, and kept that tire hard until we got just to the spot on the road where we would find what we needed, and then He lead this hunter to us to point out the tree!

Again my faith was strengthened, and since that day—yes, it would take pages to tell you "how I've proved Him o'er and o'er."

After a few days at Wukari, we proceeded (another lady missionary and myself) to Zaki Biam, one of the stations of the Dutch Reformed Church of South Africa. This trip was thirty miles, and very pleasant as we had each other for company. From there we went to Salatu, twenty-five miles, another station of Dutch Reformed Church Mission. How I enjoyed the fellowship with these friends! What a treat it was to sing the Holland psalms!

Then on the last day of February I went to Lupwe, thirty miles due south, and upon arrival sang softly, "Be it ever so humble, there's no place like home."

To be sure it was humble! It was a new station with only a few huts, most of them unfinished. The dishes were put on the dirt floor (we had as yet no beaten floor in the huts), and of course we could not boast of such luxury as a cupboard. A rope was tied from one end of the hut to the other in order that I might thus hang up some of my extra clothes. But all this did not in the least seem like inconvenience. To me this was HOME! Had not the field secretary, as soon as I arrived at Ibi, said that Takum district was to be the place where I would be stationed? Did I not look forward to coming here for one whole year?

The name of the station is Lupwe. There is no village or town right near. For health and other reasons the government has made a law that the white people have to live a certain number of yards away from any native village. This place was chosen because it seemed to be centrally located. Four miles north is Takum, the largest town in our district. This town boasts a population of three thousand, and here too lives the big chief, who has charge of all the people in this Takum district. The district is over eighty miles from north to south, with fifteen thousand people.

When erecting a new mission station, a very important item is "Can we get sufficient water?" Just near Lupwe station is a natural spring where we get all our water. The animals drink from this spring, especially in the dry season, when it is the only water available all about us. The people step into the spring with their bare feet as they dip it for us in large tins and carry it up to the compound. But for drinking purpose we boil and filter all our water.

Lupwe is beautifully situated in the midst of many hills. These are the foothills of the Cameroon mountain range. When we first came to Lupwe many of the people lived up on the top of these mountains. In this way they felt protected against the enemy. The remnant of the people, as we find them today, have survived many years of bitter tribal wars. In such wars thousands might be killed. Smallpox, influenza, and other epidemics have caused heavy and sudden decrease in the population from time to time. One may well imagine that the death rate of such a people would be high, there being no doctor or hospital, and no knowledge of the laws of sanitation and isolation. After one is a little bit acquainted with conditions it is not hard to believe the sad fact that half the children born die before they are five years old!

The name of the tribe is Dzompere, and the meaning of this name interprets to us the kind of people they are: *pere*, a man; *Dzom*, to eat; *Dzompere*, to eat a man. In plain language—Cannibals.

Due to their tribal wars, witchcraft cruelties, cannibalism, and frequent murder, the government would not readily give permission for missionaries to be stationed here. But after much prayer, the day came when that permission was granted, and soon we went to declare to these people, who so long have walked in midnight darkness, the gospel of Jesus, Who said, "I am the Light of the world."

A group of Dzompere gathered to listen to the "Story of Jesus."
See page 158.

They are a very primitive people. Never having seen white folks before, they were much afraid of us at first.

The people living among these hills wear very little or no clothing. The women generally wear great bunches of leaves, which they tie to a string of beads about the waistline. But a great many women wear nothing more than several strings of beads about the waist. The men wear a loincloth or a skin of some animal which they have killed in the bush. It may be a monkey skin or a pretty stripe covering of some antelope or small deer. The children go about, clad in their black birthday suit until ten or twelve years of age.

The people live in small, round clay huts with grass thatch roofs. A householder will have a whole cluster of tiny huts. He may have several wives, and consequently a goodly number of children, and must build sufficient huts for all his family, plus the chickens, goats, sheep, and storehut for his food.

They are a farming people, having as yet very little contact with the world outside the border of their own tribe. All the farming is done by hand with small native implements. Corn, guinea corn, sweet potato, peanuts, pumpkin, beans, and a few native vegetables are their main products. There are thousands of oil palm trees in the district, and this oil is used very freely with all their food preparations. Salt is being introduced lately, but when the people knew no salt they used ashes as a substitute for salt. Bananas (the large unsweetened kind) and pawpaw (a kind of melon) are the chief fruits grown by the natives. Much tobacco is raised and used freely by the women as well as the men. Beer is consumed in large quantities, being made from the guinea corn.

Much of the farm work is done by the men and the women together. Sometimes when a man is making a new farm, he will ask his neighbors and relatives to come and help him clear the ground of trees, stumps, stones, etc., and to turn over the soil. He cannot pay them in money, but will have several pots of beer ready, and this is reckoned as ample return for the labor given. Then the seed is planted. When the corn grows to fifteen or twenty inches above the ground, it is necessary for someone to sit in the farm to scare away the monkeys. It is a great blessing that monkeys do not come out after dark, or they might do much damage to the fields, as the people would be afraid to sit up all night to frighten them away. Three times during the season a farm is weeded. In the rainy season there is much moisture, which, together with the very great heat of the sun, causes the coarse grass and other weeds to grow with amazing speed. (There is much of this long grass in Africa during the rainy season. I have ploughed my way through some that was all of ten or twelve feet tall. When the rainy season is over, it is cut and used to make roofs for the huts.) When, finally, the corn is ripe, it is cut down, put in bundles, and carried home. Most of it is carried by the women folk. Then it is stored in a kind of clay granary, and used for food and beer.

You may be interested to know just what a woman does to keep busy all day long. She wears no clothes, and consequently does no sewing, washing, ironing and mending. Besides helping with the work of the farm and carrying the produce from the farm to their home (this is sometimes a distance of ten or twelve miles), she has the care of her children, and the grinding of all the corn, as well as the cooking of the food. She must also carry all the water that is used for cooking, drinking, and washing. She has to go out to the bush and get the firewood. She must gather what she needs for cooking, and then some spare wood for a fire by night in case it is chilly. Sleeping on a grass mat on the floor, and with no blanket, a little fire with plenty of smoke adds to their comfort. The cooking pots are made of clay, then baked, and this also belongs to the woman's share of work.

The men build the huts, cut the grass, weave some rope from the long grass or from the palm leaves, cut the bamboo sticks needed to make the frame of the roof, and after tying the frame together, and putting it in place on the clay wall of the hut, they tie the grass on, layer upon layer, making it thick enough to keep out the rain. The sleeping mats are generally woven by the men. Some build a clay bed inside the hut. Very often the men go out hunting. They make large nets (weaving the rope themselves) and take along spears and bow and arrows. Quite frequently a leopard trap is made, and many a wild beast has been speared to death after getting itself caught in such a trap.

Any kind of meat is acceptable to the natives. Rats and ants are roasted and eaten. Lizard, large non-poisonous snake, monkey, dog, lion, leopard, buffalo, and hippopotamus are never to be despised. They are all considered a "rare treat."

Arriving at our station Lupwe, my home, and taking note of the humble mud huts dotted over that compound, I said,

> "A hut, or a mansion, what matter where?
> Where Jesus is, 'tis heaven there."

But it was not long before I found out that, outside the walls of our hut, there was nothing to remind us of heaven.

The darkness that reigned throughout that district was appalling! At times it seemed to crush me on every side! It is a sickening sight to see a host of heathen dancing and drinking beer until they get to that pitch where passion and lust have full control.

Besides this particular tribe, the Dzompere, we had in our district that large town of Takum, with the Mohammedan settlement and a large majority of Jukun. Towards the south could be found a few more towns like this, with a predominant Jukun population and a small Mohammedan settlement. North of Takum, but within the border of our district, were two more towns of like nature. The Jukun is a very large tribe to the north and east of us. It has a distinct language of its own.

Summing up the district we were responsible for a territory eighty miles long, with fifteen thousand people, representing the entire Dzompere tribe, a few thousand of the Jukun tribe, and some Mohammedans.

This was the first mission station opened in this district and we were the first white people to be stationed here.

Would we ever, in this district, among this cannibal people, see the prophecy fulfilled, "The people that walked in darkness have seen a great light—they that dwell in the land of the shadow of death, upon them hath the light shined"?

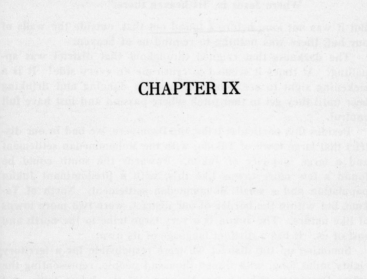

CHAPTER IX

"The Spirit of the Lord is upon me, because He hath anointed me to preach the gospel to the poor; He hath sent me to heal the broken-hearted, to preach deliverance to the captives, and recovering of sight to the blind, to set at liberty them that are bruised."

CHAPTER IX

THE POWER OF SPIRIT WORSHIP

For many long centuries the great heart of Africa has been bound with strong coils of fetishism. Millions of people have been born, gone through life, and died, without knowing anything higher than the dreadful fear of "spirit worship."

In this world there are many false religions. Every such false religion is a product of the bottomless pit. And in Africa millions of pagan people are slaves to the false religion which we term "fetishism." And fetishism is nothing more and nothing less than spirit worship. There are "good spirits" and "evil spirits."

It is not possible for me to give a detailed report of this pagan worship. Every tribe seems to have its own peculiar system, and only the older men of the tribe are let in on the secrets of how the spirits work. Should such an old man, or a "witch-doctor" be converted, one might get to know a great deal about this spirit worship. It is also necessary that one have opportunity to compare the system of one tribe with that of another. A most thorough knowledge of the language is demanded to understand the intricate detail of fetishism. One might be excused from all missionary work and devote a lifetime to the study of this religious system. My own experience has been far too short and too limited to dwell at length on the matter.

However, this one thing I do know, that spirit worship is full of idolatry, witchcraft, superstition and fear. I might give you a few illustrations which have crossed the path of my own experience.

In the month of April I went to a certain village. During this month we frequently have very heavy tornado storms. Two men were walking along the path and were killed in such a storm. The lightning struck a hut in the village and four people were killed. Quite naturally the people are afraid of these storms. I noticed that outside the huts were two short poles; one a straight pointed pole, the other close beside it a forked pole. I asked what these poles meant, and was told that they were the spirits guarding the hut and protecting the inmates against the tornado storms. The straight pointed pole was the female spirit and the forked pole was the male spirit. At that same village I went to another compound and saw a large clay image of a beast. I asked the meaning of this, and was told that this spirit was to keep away the leopards.

The mother of one of the boys in our boarding school was coming along the path from the farm to her own compound, a distance of some ten miles. She was not far away from the mission station when suddenly she found herself surrounded by several men, who began to dance and sing, saying, "We have found meat." The men were cannibals. Though frightened, she was calm enough to tell a lie. She said to these men: "You think I am alone, but I am not alone, my husband is on the path and a little behind me." Then the human flesh hunters ran off for fear their faces would be seen by a man, and they be asked to appear and give account before the big chief of the district. Of course the woman told her husband, and they tried to get the men, but were not successful. Some time afterward this woman had a bitter quarrel with her husband. She ran away from him, and was purposing to come to her son at our mission station. On her way, two men of the village met her, and taking her, one by each hand, led her back to her enraged husband. Then the husband said, "She is bewitched. She has an evil spirit." Once a woman is told that she possesses an evil spirit, and, especially if that statement comes from the lips of her husband, she has no more desire to live. The next morning a message came to us that this woman was dead. She had committed suicide. In a small hut that was not used often, she was found hanging on a rope. She reasoned thus: "My husband has declared that I am possessed of an evil spirit; quite likely I shall soon be killed; it is better that I die at once."

Many a little present had this woman given me when I visited their compound. Upon my last visit she ran down from the top of the hill, dressed in her garment of leaves, and came and sat just close beside me. She had a lovely clean body, a bright cheerful countenance, and it seemed to me that her eyes sparkled with affection and delight. And I can truthfully say that my heart was warm with love to this woman. As I mounted that hill, and stood beside her grave, I wept at the thought of the heavy quota of lives sacrificed to this cruel system of witchcraft.

I walked over to a high rocky place where stood a very large tree. From this spot I got a delightful view of the mountains for several miles before me. As I stood there, gazing upon thousands of flourishing green palms, and upon equally many grass-capped huts, my soul was lifted above these towering mountains. I yearned for the day when God would speak, and say to these people: "Let there be light!"

The ground on which I then stood was a sacred spot, the big tree was a spirit tree; upon these rocks human lives have been sacrificed!

Not many years ago—within the lifetime of the Christian who told me this, and who witnessed it with his own eyes—two women were killed by order of the witch-doctor. It happened on this very hill. A terrible calamity came to the people of this hill. And the question immediately arose: "Who is to blame for this evil?" As usual, the witch-doctor was consulted. He accused two women. At a certain appointed time they were brought to the place of sacrifice. A group of men formed a kind of circle. The women were commanded to dance. As they danced hot irons or hot spears were touched against their naked body to brand them. Exhausted with pain and terror and dancing they fell to the ground. They were then tied to a palm tree and speared to death. Lest the evil spirit within them should escape or be committed to a leopard, should the beast come by night and bite from the corpse, the bodies were burned to ashes.

After the Christian youth told me this pathetic story, I asked him whether they would only kill *women* in this manner. Did the witch-doctor never pronounce judgment upon a *man*. The answer I got was this: "It sometimes happens that a man is killed in some such cruel way, but when they thus kill a man, they first give him plenty of beer to drink. Then when he is full of beer, he does not feel much pain. But a woman must drink the whole measure of pain."

Should a woman expect to give birth to a child, she is urged to bring gifts of food and beer, or a fowl or goat, to the spirit house, and thus receive help in her hour of need. Such food, of course, is consumed by the witch-doctor and his friends. After the birth of a child, a mother is expected to bring more gifts in order to keep the spirits from getting angry and causing the death of her child.

As soon as a person is afflicted with any sickness, the witch-doctor is consulted and whatever sacrifice he prescribes is brought at once.

When a person dies, again gifts are brought to the spirit

Virgin country with spirit hut in the foreground.   See page 97.

house. At certain set periods there will be a dance to mourn the dead, especially in the case of a householder or a married woman who has ever borne a son. At such a dance many gallons of beer will be consumed. The spirit-man will bring messages from the dead person. Such a dance was once going on right near my hut. A Christian man was with me on the veranda, telling me the meaning of the weird sounds. "Now the 'Boka' (spirit-man) is telling the wives of the dead man what he wants them to bring. The dead man says he wants a sleeping mat, and a blanket, as he is cold." After the dance is over (it may last three or seven days and nights) the women will work to get the sleeping mat and covering, and send it to the spirit house.

I told you that the big chief lives in Takum, four miles from Lupwe. This chief has between ninety and a hundred wives. The chief himself is a heathen, though he comes often to our chapel, and he brings me a friendly call occasionally, and often sends to ask me to give him medicine, or for some other help. I have had many services in his compound, and have repeatedly dealt with him personally regarding his soul. One of his many wives is a Christian. She belongs to our little flock of believers, though as yet she is not baptized. Last year she came to me after a Sunday service. She looked sad and acted rather nervous. She was carrying a heavy burden; I greeted her cordially, and then invited her to unburden her heart to me. It was a rather long story. For nearly two months the chief had been sick. At first the spirits were consulted and they said that one of the many wives of the chief was possessed of an evil spirit and was passing it on to her husband, and this accounted for his sickness. "Which wife can it be? There are so many." A test was to be applied to all to find out who was the guilty one. There are different tests. One is to wash the eyes with ground red pepper. Who suffers most is the guilty one. Whatever was the test on this particular occasion, I do not know. I felt led not to ask. But Z—— (the Christian wife) at first refused, saying that she believed in Jesus, and could have nothing to do with the spirits. At once they said, "Then you are the guilty person. You refuse the test. That proves you have given this sickness to your husband!" This thoroughly frightened her; she lost courage, and permitted herself to be numbered with her many sisters in polygamy and receive the test. Weeks went by. The chief did not get better. A witch-doctor from a place several miles away was brought in to see if he could help. He too declared that one of the many wives was to blame. A second test was ordered. Z——, with the other sin still unconfessed, had no power to resist, and for a second time she permitted herself to be put through this heathen performance. So she said to me on this particular Sunday: "I have committed a great sin. My heart has lost all its peace. Through fear I denied Jesus, and now He is angry with me. I want to confess my sin publicly. Maybe the Lord will forgive and accept me, and give me peace once again." Big tears fell from her eyes to the grass mat on which she sat. I spoke softly to her of Him Who is ready to forgive if we confess our sin. We knelt together and prayed. Then I kissed her, and she passed out of the hut to go home. During the afternoon service she came to the front in the little chapel, and stood there, making public confession of her sin, and pleading with the other Christians and missionary to forgive her and to pray for her.

> "O Holy Father, through the merit of Jesus
> Christ, and His finished work on Calvary, come
> to lift these heavy burdens; release these people
> from the captivity of spirit worship, and set
> them gloriously free in the liberty of the Holy
> Spirit. Amen."

CHAPTER X

In the purpose of God stands the triumph of Christ,
  The end is assured for the word has been spoken:
His promise for yesterday's victory sufficed:
  It holds for today, and shall never be broken.
Forth then in faith! Be thou faithful to death,
And expect the fulfilment of all that He saith!
  Though against thee should rise all the powers of hell,
  We hail Thee world's Victor—O Immanuel!

CHAPTER X

THE MORAL LIFE OF THE DZOMPERE

From the two foregoing chapters you may conclude that the moral life of these people is very low. It will not do to rashly pull aside the curtain and let you see the depth to which these people have sunk in their social contacts. It is a delicate subject and one must needs tread carefully. On the other hand, we must tear away the cloak of false modesty, in order to understand how tremendous is the task confronting the Christian missionary; and in order to have stimulated within us a deeper desire for the salvation of the heathen, as well as a quickened note of praise for all the blessings that are ours in Christ Jesus our Lord.

Among a people like the Dzompere, where there is so much nakedness, where shame and modesty are practically unknown, where the eyes and ears of tiny children are permitted to see and hear such things as we would consider unlawful; where passion knows no restraint, it is fitting to apply the words of Scripture: "And God saw that the wickedness of man was great in the earth, and that every imagination of the thoughts of his heart was only evil continually."

There are certain diseases which are the direct result of immorality. Such diseases abound in nearly every heathen land. In our part of Africa, due to such diseases, a great percentage of the women go through life childless. It may or it may not be her own fault, but she is always told that she is herself to blame if she does not bear her husband a son. Consequently, if a man marries, and the woman does not have a child, he sets out to seek another wife. Should this second wife have children, she will be the "well-favored" one, and upon her he may lavish many gifts and most of his attention. Pity the poor woman who is slighted, offended and ignored all her life because she is childless!

In our tribe it is customary for a woman to isolate herself at certain set periods. She is not to enter the hut of her husband, nor to touch any of the utensils used for cooking or carrying water. She is not to prepare or cook any food. At such a time, who is to do the cooking? Who is to draw the water? With this system of polygamy, a man can have one of his wives on duty all the time, and so this difficulty is overcome.

Because the big chief has nearly a hundred wives, and the minor chiefs have anywhere from four to twenty, and several of the so-called "big men" have four or six, and a host of men have two, it stands to reason that there must be a shortage of women. Some men may seek a wife for years and not be able to find one. This leads to unspeakable sin. Such unmarried men go about enticing the women who are married to polygamists. All too many of these married women, because they receive so little attention from their own husband, yield readily to temptation from without.

There are different marriage customs. A man of power, such as a chief, may force any girl to enter his compound and become

Two Christian lads with a patient at the dispensary and two of his children. The little girl with uplifted hand, is about ten years old, and the man's third wife. See page 103.

his wife. Sometimes a girl is consulted as to whether she is willing to marry a certain man. Sometimes she is forced against her will to become the virgin-bride of some old man. In such a case it is her father or brother who makes the arrangement for her.

Among the Dzompere, there are two common customs. The one is to *buy* a wife. The other is to get a wife by *exchange*. Let me illustrate:

One day the father of one of our Christian schoolboys sent a message to me to send his son home at once. I did so, of course. That day the father presented his son (a lad of about fifteen) with a little girl-wife (a child of about thirteen). The father bought this little girl, paying the regular dowry for her. The price paid was thirty sheep or goats. The parents of this little girl will not be able to ask her back because they will have consumed some of the dowry, and some of the goats or sheep will have died. This is the best marriage custom because a man is quite sure of being able to keep his wife. She is his possession.

That same father also gave to another son a present of a wife. But this woman was not bought with a dowry. This woman had already been married four times. The father exchanged one of his own wives for this one. He was getting old, and wanted to see his sons well provided for. But this marriage by exchange leads to no end of trouble and difficulty. Later on, the wife was taken and exchanged again for a smaller girl, and this little girl cried so much that she had to be taken back to her parents. Soon this son was left without a wife at all. The system of exchange leads to gross immorality.

A heathen man from a neighboring village came to our dispensary. He was on our compound for a time. He had two wives and a few children with him. There was also a shy little girl of about ten years old. I asked him: "Is this nice girl your daughter?" With a broad smile he answered, "That is my wife also." He had a quarrel with his former third wife because she fell in love with another man. He took the matter to the native court, and it was decided that the third wife remain with the man whom she loved, but that this man pay the price—a little girl—to the offended husband. So here beside him stood the little girl of ten—his wife.

A prominent path goes by our compound. It is what one might call "the highway," as it passes through several tribes and leads to the trading center—seventy-five miles from our station. Several men come along this path to go to Takum, where they find food and rest in a large native market. The Christians tell me that ten years ago no woman would dare to walk this path alone from Lupwe to Takum, four miles distance. They would surely be approached by the men traveling on this path, and there would be no way of escape.

Two miles from us is a large hill with fifteen hundred people. There are thousands of palm trees. At a certain season these trees are tapped, and palm wine is extracted. This wine is very sweet and ferments easily. After twenty-four hours it is like whisky or gin. Many women come from Takum, pass by our compound to go to this hill for palm wine. They take it back to Takum and sell it in the market there. How much do they pay for this wine? The evangelist working in our district told me that no man who cares for his wife will permit her to be a "wine-hauler," because the palm wine is bought from the hill men for the price of sin.

I have told you only a very little bit. You can understand how these conditions drag a people down. And you may know what a terrible struggle it is for the converts, considering the downward pull of heredity and tribal customs. The gospel of Jesus Christ is the only power that will enable them to rise to any standard of purity. The wonderful change wrought in the lives of several who have come out of this darkness and immorality into the blessed light of the Savior is the great challenge to the missionary to continue and "fight the good fight of faith!"

CHAPTER XI

"The angel of the Lord encampeth round about them that fear him, and delivereth them."

CHAPTER XI

"IN PERILS IN THE WILDERNESS"—I

Of the immense variety of insects in Central Africa, the mosquito is probably the most dreaded by the missionaries. There is a great deal of malaria among the natives. Many young children go about with distended abdomen, due to enlarged spleen, caused by malaria. Though the mortality among the people is exceedingly high, it is nevertheless true that they can survive a fever that would kill any white person. Malaria being so common, most of the mosquitoes become infected. In this way they pass on the malaria germ. Fever has caused the death of many white people, officials and traders, as well as missionaries. The entire west coast of Africa has been rightly called "the white man's grave." For this reason we are obliged to take five grains of quinine daily (increasing the dose as soon as symptoms of fever arise); wear leather mosquito boots in the evening (these boots come to the knees, thus protecting the ankles and lower limbs from the insect bites); and every night of the year we sleep under the protection of mosquito net. This net is fastened to the top of the bed and tucked in all around the mattress. One night I tried to sleep without this net, but, not having a wink of sleep by midnight, I was forced to get up, find a net and fasten it on the bed.

Mosquitoes are also believed to carry the germ of yellow fever—a tropical disease that has caused the death of not a few white people in Africa.

Of course we have the common house fly. All food must be kept covered, and protected against any germ that this fly may carry. Leprosy is common, sore eyes and open ulcers abound, and the germ of these diseases may be easily carried by a fly.

We also have the tsetse fly, which carries the sleeping sick
ness germ. Many of the Africans are afflicted with this dread
ful disease, that has always meant sure death to them. Of late
there is a serum used and a few white people have recovered
from sleeping sickness. Due to this tsetse fly we are not able
to have cattle in the district where I work, as they easily become
infected and die off with sleeping sickness.

There are a great variety of other small insects, quite harm
less but sometimes very annoying. Due to the intense heat of
the tropics, and the fact that we never have a frost, insects abound
in great numbers and multiply rapidly.

Many different kinds of ants are to be seen. The ones that
pester us the most are the "driver ant" and the "white ant." The
driver ant is like a regiment of soldiers, and moves from one
place to another. Should they choose to pass through your hut
you are obliged to vacate until the last of the regiment has gone
by. One evening I came home and stood drinking a glass of
water. I stood right in the ant trail, without knowing it, of
course, and pretty soon I felt myself bitten by these little enemies
I hurried to get a lantern and found the floor black with ants
My interference had caused a break in their chain, which they
were now trying to mend. There was no remedy but to leave
them alone. Truly there were thousands and thousands of them
There was one continual stream of ants all night and the whole
next morning. Having passed through, my place was as clear of
ants as before they entered.

The white ant lives on building material. Through the mud
walls of our hut, they build a tunnel and thus get passage to the
roof. Once in the roof, they stay there. They thrive on the bamboo poles of which the roof frame is made and also eat the
grass. They get into the wooden door frame, and very soon you
will have only an empty shell instead of a heavy piece of lumber.
One night a missionary and his wife stayed at our place. She
hung an undergarment on a nail of the door. By morning she
was not able to wear the garment, it was so thoroughly eaten
by white ants. On one of our treks through a part of the district,
I slept in a tumble-down shack, alive with white ants, and during

a single night they nearly ate the bottom out of one of my boxes. We keep everything raised from the floor on bricks or tins for protection against these white ants.

Another unwelcome little creature is the centipede. It is a caterpillar-like insect, with a shell back, rather flat body, and many legs along both sides of its body. They range from three to six inches long. I remember my first experience with such an intruder. It was in the morning. I was at prayer, and heard a crawling noise on the grass mat where I was kneeling. I looked, and saw this "funny worm." I took off my bedroom slipper, and slapped it a few times, and continued my devotions. Soon it wiggled again, and I got a piece of paper, took hold of it, and walked outside to the other missionary who was just on the path. "Here is something for you to dissect," I said, "seeing you are so interested in bugs!" "Drop it quickly, you foolish girl, it is a centipede!" he exclaimed, and went on to tell about them and their mean sting. At another town, while nursing one of our missionaries, I found a centipede on my clothes while I was dressing one morning. We have killed quite a few at Lupwe.

The scorpion is also a much dreaded little fellow. He has a sharp stinger at the end of his tail, and when stinging a person, he injects a poison which causes terrific pain. There are different kinds of scorpions, small and large. One sting is mild, causing pain for about three to five hours; but another scorpion will cause intense agony for three days. We have killed many of these at Lupwe, and the natives tell us that the large coarse black ones often cause death.

Lizards are also plentiful. There are many different varieties of these. They play tag freely inside and about our huts, and are perfectly harmless.

During the first few months we were at Lupwe we caught not less than forty rats in my two huts. Some evenings we would set the traps two or three times over before nine o'clock. Now we keep a pussy to help us out of this difficulty. There are many rats in the bush all about us. They are of the same size as a house rat, but with darker skin, and coarser flesh. The natives go out to hunt these and consider them a rare delicacy. A village chief once presented me with a big bush rat, which had just been captured that afternoon. I did gather enough courage to eat the hind quarter, and must admit that it tasted just as good as mutton!

We now pass on to the most dreaded of all creeping creatures, the snake. I have already told you how the bite of a small black snake caused the death of a lady missionary just after I entered Africa. At that time a missionary said to me, "You are new in the country. Let me tell you something. Never step from the bed with your bare feet on the floor. First put on your mosquito boots. And keep them up from the ground on a chair beside the bed. You never know how near a scorpion or snake may be." Now it is true that we do not see these crawling things every day in Africa. But it is equally true that they are there, hiding in their nests, or lurking about in the bush, and it does pay to exercise care.

It was some months after I was in Africa before I killed a snake. One evening a convert was with me for a personal talk. I was living alone in a large school room at the time, and doing language study. The boy sat on a grass mat on the floor, and I was on a folding chair. All of a sudden I said, "Stand up, S——, a snake is coming toward you!" I also arose and stood with both feet on the snake, which was about fifteen inches long, while S—— got a board with which to kill it. I asked him was it a poisonous kind, and he said he could not tell. I put it in a corner of the big room, placed a board over it, and a weight on the board, intending to show it to one of the other missionaries the next day. We finished our talk, and S—— got up to go to his hut. I left the door open, so the light of the lanterns would shine outside, and he would not need to be afraid. The door would not shut easily, and I pressed against it with my shoulder. As I did so, a snake fell from the roof on my hand. I shook it off to the ground, ran for the board and killed it. It was the same size and color as the other, so I concluded they must be "twins" and that there might be a nest in the roof. That night I tossed for hours, unable to get to sleep. It was my first dealing with snakes, and I was so conscious of their lying dead on the floor in yonder corner of the room. I was also fearing lest there might be more crawling about.

Since then I have killed quite a number of snakes, and, while I know I shall never enjoy their company, I am not so nervous about them as at first.

One evening we sat outside enjoying a lovely moonlight rest. I called out to my co-worker, who was with me, "Stand up quickly, a snake is just crawling under your chair." We called for lantern and club but the snake beat us to the bush and got lost in the grass. Another day we were on trek in the bush. We were in a hut and had just finished our noon meal. I looked about, and three feet away, just beside my campbed was a snake over a yard long. As I stirred to get something, he lifted his head, turned about and was out of the hut in a flash. We failed to get it.

At Lupwe we have a cup of tea every day at four o'clock, after school is out. My co-worker looked up and said, "Why there's a snake in our roof." We hurried out and by means of a native implement there held it against the grass of the roof. It was a long, thin, slimy, green-black specimen, such as I had not seen before. But the grass being soft, the snake wiggled itself free and was soon lost to our sight. We had to return to our tea, and be content to know that it was hiding somewhere in our roof.

Let me finish by telling you of the biggest snake I have ever seen in Africa. One Saturday afternoon the school boys and workmen went out hunting. There is ample opportunity for this sport all about Lupwe station. About a quarter of a mile from the mission station, a boy spied a python, lying all coiled up and asleep on the sand. Having his spear with him, he hurled it at the head of the python, pinning it to the ground. Then he yelled for the others to come, and soon there was much rejoicing at this great "find." The python was compelled to lie quietly due to the fact that it had swallowed a small antelope just the day before. This animal lay intact inside the python, causing the body of the python to be much distended at that certain spot. Hence the snake was unable to move about until this little deer could be digested. The python was all of three yards long, and the little deer inside was all of twenty to thirty pounds. It seems natural for a snake to slowly take in a whole animal, rather than chew it to pieces or swallow it bit by bit. I have seen a smaller snake with a whole frog inside of it. They seem to have a good deal of elasticity in their muscles. Well, our boys carried the python to the mission station. They came in singing for joy, and I went out to see what it was all about. There lay the python; there lay the little deer, without a broken bone, and with spots of its brown hairy covering still showing. This proved that it had only been devoured the day before. There were also more than thirty eggs inside the python. And what a feast our people did have! Deer, python, eggs—every bit was eaten! As they gathered around their supper that evening they offered the doxology of praise, to thank the Creator for His rich provision!

And now, dear friend, I hope you have not read this chapter before going to bed, lest your sleep be disturbed by exciting dreams. The next chapter will be related to this, dealing with the bigger animals, and I would advise you to read it in the day time if you are not inclined to have your sleep interrupted by reading such incidents as these.

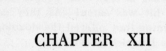

CHAPTER XII

*"The Lord is thy keeper . . .
The Lord shall preserve thy going
out and thy coming in from this
time forth, and even forevermore."*

CHAPTER XII

"IN PERILS IN THE WILDERNESS"—II

You have heard of Roosevelt and others going to Africa to hunt big game. You may have visited the zoo and have seen some of these African animals at close range. To see them behind heavy bars is indeed fascinating. How intensely interesting it is to visit the zoo at feeding time! What large quantities of meat are thrown into the cages and ravenously consumed by the wild animals! And how daintily a monkey will pick up a banana and peel it!

But away out in the jungles of that great continent there are no iron bars to keep the tigers from prowling about. There are no keepers to go and feed the lions at set times. And being so far removed from the railway, and from a doctor, there are not many big game hunters who come our way. I have yet to see or hear of the first one. True it is, most of our men missionaries keep a rifle and go hunting for a bit of recreation. Many people have asked me whether I did not keep a revolver with me all the time. For one year I had a rifle, and scurried about the neighborhood a few times. After a year's play at this game, I had one single trophy—a monkey! With a shotgun I had brought down several birds. But for the last three years I have had no ambition along this line, and did not possess a gun of any kind.

It is my purpose here to tell you only of such animals as are found in our own district.

If we could make ourselves believe that we are closely related to the monkey, that they are our honorable ancestors, we should never feel lonely in Africa's big bush. There are thousands of monkeys to keep us company. Fact is, however, that when they enter the cornfield of our compound, we drive them away as

[115]

quickly as possible. One day, coming up the path on my bicycle
I counted all of thirteen monkeys—baby ones and full-grown
parents—jump quickly out of the farm and across the path into
the wild bush on the other side. Just near us is a hill called
Beka. As we sit out in the evening we can hear them bark and
quarrel, great squads of them. There are many caves along this
mountain, and here they make their home. From the top of the
mountain down to a stream they have made a path, which is so
prominent that it can be seen quite a long way off. There are
several of the large baboons, and the natives are generally afraid
of these. The monkey is a vegetarian animal, but it has happened that they kill a human being. Should one try to steal one
of their babies, danger would be near. They twist their tail
tightly about a person's ankles, thus checking the circulation.

All about us are herds of deer and antelope. We see these
quite frequently. They are very timid, and perfectly harmless.
It is lovely to see a big deer, with great horns on his head
standing by the side of the path, or gently walking into the
compound.

Until just recently I did not know that we ever had lions in
the district. It being a hilly country all around, I was told that
lions would not be found as they chose to live on the plains.
However, a missionary was going from Lupwe to Takum on
Sunday morning for the services which are held there regularly,
and saw two lions standing in the bush quite near. Just about
that time two black men were killed by some wild animal about
six miles from our mission station.

And it was not until two years ago that I knew we had wild
buffalo roaming about in our district. It is a great blessing that
one does not meet all these friends in a single day! I was about
forty miles from the mission station, on a tour through part of
the district. At a certain village we had services and stopped
to sleep. The next morning we were on our way to another village. Traveling on the bicycle, I would keep well ahead of the
men who were carrying the loads. Being alone, and early in
the morning, I was singing while riding along. The path was
narrow, and had many curves. I happened to look up and there

ust about twenty yards away, stood some great big animals, which I thought were cows. A cattle trader, having a few cows, had slept at the same village where we spent the previous night. Hence I concluded that these were his cows. I rang the bell of the bicycle repeatedly, and they jumped away. Still I rode on, entirely ignorant of the fact that I was in real danger. But a second time these beasts stood before me, and this time I saw them more clearly than before. There was not so much thick grass. Then I saw that they were bigger than cows, and their great eyes and horns gave me a sudden shock. I pressed and pressed the bicycle bell, ringing it furiously, and a second time they jumped away. I did not dare to go on. Nor had I the courage to turn around and retrace my steps. I was afraid that they might run in a circle and meet me a third time. I shook with fear, and prayed that the Lord would soon send someone along the path. It was not long before my personal boy and the native evangelist came to where I stood. I told them what had happened, and from the tracks of the beasts they knew at once that it was a herd of wild buffalo. Then they told me that on several occasions before buffalo had been seen in that region. They told me how, if angry, the buffalo would throw a person in the air with his great horns. I did not again get on the wheel that morning, but walked along with the folk who were accompanying me on this trek.

There are two rivers in our district. One is called the Gamana, and the other, the larger, is called the Katsina Allah River. It is believed that nearly all the rivers in Central Africa contain crocodiles. Being in a canoe one is protected against these. But it happens sometime that a person bathing in the river will have a leg or hand snapped off by this reptile. For this reason the white people never bathe or swim in the rivers.

In the Katsina Allah River two missionaries came to meet a very tragic death. They belonged to the Dutch Reformed Church of South Africa, which works among the large Munchi tribe, adjoining the Dzompere. Two of their single men missionaries, out on their first term of service, were crossing the river in a native canoe. When well into the river, a large hippopotamus ap-

proached their canoe. One of the men fired a shot from his rifle
which failed to strike the hippo in a fatal spot. Instead, it likely
angered him, and he swam up close to the canoe, put his big
square mouth underneath and turned the canoe upside down. The
natives who were in the canoe swam to shore quickly. The
missionaries were at a disadvantage, as they had on heavy shoes
and a cartridge belt loaded with shot. They did not get to shore
In the twinkling of an eye they reached yonder Golden Shore
that borders the City Four-Square. Other missionaries were
sent for and watched the banks of the river; the government
officials were notified and they placed men on guard. After
few days four pieces of human body were found. The hippo
with his great mouth, had severed each body clean in half, and
here were the four parts of the two bodies of these missionaries
They were so badly mangled that it could not be seen which was
which. But a coffin was made to contain the remains, and

African buffalo. See page 116.

uneral was held, and for the first time the missionaries of the
Dutch Reformed Church of South Africa, working among the
Munchi in the great Sudan, stood around the open graves of two
of their fellow workers.

The field is so great, the workers so few; we cannot understand why they must be taken away in their first term of service.
We bow in submission and say,

> "O Will, that willest good alone,
> Lead Thou the way, Thou guidest best."

Several of the Dzompere people have been killed by leopards.
The many hills and mountains about us contain a goodly number
of caves where the leopards may dwell and safely protect their
young. By day they sleep and rarely leave their place of hiding.
By night they come forth and prowl about in search of food.
Many a deer is sleeping in the open under the canopy of heaven.
And the leopards go out in search of these tame animals. They
will also enter the compounds in search of dogs, sheep or goats.
Our boys once found a large deer, weighing well over a hundred
pounds, lying dead in the grass near our place. The leopard had
killed it, but failed to drag it away.

Many an evening we hear the howl of the leopard in our
neighborhood. Having heard the long piercing groan of a lion,
the "laughing" of the hyena, and the broken howl of the leopard,
we are able to know at once which animal it is that is prowling
about. But very often they enter the compound by night and we
never hear them. They go about from hut to hut, stealthily, in
quiet search of something to eat, leaving behind their footprints
to tell us of their night time visits.

"Why do you not build a heavy wall about the compound?"
a kind friend asked me one day. This would be the only remedy
to keep out such wild animals. But while we would thus lock
ourselves in, we would shut out the people who come to us for
medical treatment, for a little trading, for a friendly greeting.
We are so glad to have them come in, but they would be afraid
to enter if we put up a high wall. So it is a case of "taking the
bitter with the sweet."

One night I slept in the school hut. There were no doors so I fastened grass mats to the openings, as a kind of protection These mats were short and only reached to within about twenty inches from the ground. I had just gone to bed, when I heard a scratching outside the door on the path. At once I surmised that it might be a leopard. I lay very quietly, though fear caused me to breathe quickly and heavily. Again I asked the Lord to undertake and protect me. The scratching ceased, and I fell asleep. In the morning we saw the paw marks of the leopard all about the doorway.

Last year we had a very large leopard come into our com pound several nights in succession. He never made a sound, bu each morning we saw the fresh paw marks.

One morning, before six o'clock, one of the boys came to me and said, "White lady, did you see these marks outside your veranda?" I went to look, and there were several monstrous paw marks. The leopard had been right upon my veranda, just near the bedroom window. All night the shutters were wide open, and the window is low so as to let in plenty of air. There was no screen or glass. Very easily the beast could have stepped inside. As it jumped down from the veranda, it pulled along three heavy stones. The wall is made of stones mudded together (as you will see from the picture of my house). What caused this beast to turn away and jump down from the veranda, rather than enter my hut? The guardian angel of the Lord may have sent it away. The Bible assures us that there are ministering angels sent from the realms above to protect the children of God

May the Lord increase our faith to believe that our Jehovah never changeth! He sealed the mouth of the lions to protect Daniel; He stood beside the three men in the fiery furnace, and we may believe that He still stands beside His missionary servants in the far-away, isolated and dangerous places of "earth's harvest fields so wide."

CHAPTER XIII

"Study . . . to show thyself approved unto God."

CHAPTER XIII

THE TASK OF A PIONEER MISSIONARY

In February, 1922, I left Lupwe to come home on furlough, after having been in Africa two years. Our terms of service are short, due to the fact that the Benue valley is considered one of the most deadly places in the world for white people. Isolation, tornado storms, insects and wild beasts, fever and overwork all help to cause the nervous system to suffer continual strain.

Shortly after I left, Rev. and Mrs. Whitman had to come home for furlough, and there were no missionaries to be sent to Lupwe. The station, so newly opened, was left for nine months without a resident missionary.

On February 1, 1923, I returned for my second term of service. The Whitmans were not able to go back to the field, due to ill health. Neither did the mission have another ordained man to put in charge of this Takum district. It was decided that two women would be stationed at Lupwe to take up and continue the work there.

For the first three months I was alone, and then Miss Haigh returned from furlough in England and joined me at Lupwe.

What was our task? To bring the gospel to fifteen thousand people scattered over an area of eighty miles from north to south.

Just what does that involve? It meant that we would be obliged to do *intensive* and *extensive* mission work. By *intensive* work, we mean all that is done within the confines of our mission compound. By *extensive* mission work is meant all that we do for the spread of the gospel outside the limit of our compound, and as far as the border line of our district.

There is so much *intensive* work that one has continually to guard against that temptation that comes to the missionary to stick in one place—home, and neglect the miles of territory about him. On the station we have our own home which includes the regular household routine. We also have a dispensary where patients come each morning to receive medical help. A station school is conducted for the people residing on the compound. New huts have to be erected; leaking grass roofs have to be torn down and new ones put on. A compound comprising five acres of ground has to be kept in good order and ready for inspection whenever an official comes to visit the district. Besides this are reports, accounts, and mail. From day to day palavers arise. Some can be settled in a few minutes; others take hours, and the big ones often consume days of a missionary's time. By palaver we mean matters of discipline.

The *extensive* work, however, is so very important that one cannot afford to neglect it. Four miles from Lupwe is Takum,

A leopard in the wilderness. See page 119.

the largest town of our district. Here we have an out-station.
We have a chapel where regular services are held each Sunday.
Every Thursday morning a prayer meeting is called at eight
o'clock. At Takum we have a small group of Christians, who at
present form the nucleus of our little flock. These Christians must
be taught to read and write, so we must give them school; they
must have catechism instruction, in order that they may receive
the sacrament of baptism in due time; many hours must be
spent in personal work. These Christians are babes in Christ;
they frequently stumble, and sometimes they fall deep into gross
sin. Then the missionary has to probe, rebuke, admonish, and
convincingly urge these who have offended God's law to repent
and make public confession. Such matters of discipline demand
hours of time, endless patience, the wisdom of the Holy Spirit,
and an inexhaustible supply of love.

Though Takum is the largest town in the district, it is nevertheless only one place. There are very many more towns, hills
and villages where we must visit and tell the people the ever-
lasting gospel of the Eternal God. Several of these places can be
reached in a day. That is, the missionary can go in the morning,
and return home in the evening. But by far the majority of
people can be reached only a few times a year when the missionary is touring through the district. In the remote places of the
district they may hear only once a year.

Out of the three hundred and sixty-five days of last year, I
spent more than two hundred away from the compound, in
extensive mission work.

The pioneer missionary is, of course, expected to continue
his language study.

The work might be accomplished with greater speed if we
had a trained force of native teachers and evangelists. That is
exactly the lack in pioneer work. We must wait until some
converts are won, and then call from among them a given number who seem to be spiritually keen and intellectually bright,
and train them to become leaders. And this in itself is a
tremendous task, the training of Christian teachers and evan-

gelists, that could easily absorb the total effort of two missionaries.

Surely it is unwise ever to come before a class unprepared.
I feel it is a great wrong to go and conduct a Bible class, catechism, or prayer meeting, without having a preparatory period
of study. I dare not go to morning chapel worship and read the
the Holy Scriptures unless I have first read over the portion in
my own room.

And can we effectually talk to others about God unless we have
first spoken to the Lord about them? Must we not have a daily
period of Bible study, prayer and meditation? Is the missionary
not grieved when the converts fall into flagrant sin? And in
such cases, will he not feel the urge to special periods of intercession—possibly with fasting?

You will not judge it a *light* task that confronts the foreign
missionary who is called upon to do pioneer service.

And for this task, as I have tried to outline it in this chapter,
we two women workers were responsible. I am more than willing
to admit that we failed to accomplish *all* our task.

Hippopotamus. See page 117.

CHAPTER XIV

."He was not willing that any should perish;"
  Jesus enthroned in the glory above,
 Saw our poor fallen world, pitied our sorrows,
  Poured out His life for us, wonderful love!
 Perishing! Perishing! thronging our pathway,
  Hearts break with burdens too heavy to bear,
 Jesus would save, but there's no one to tell them,
  No one to lift them from sin and despair.

 "He was not willing that any should perish;"
  Cloth'd in our flesh with its sorrow and pain,
 Came He to seek the lost, comfort the mourner,
  Heal the heart-broken by sorrow and shame.
 Perishing! Perishing! harvest is passing,
  Reapers are few, and the night draweth near;
 Jesus is calling thee, haste to the reaping,
  Thou shalt have souls, precious souls, for thy hire.

 Plenty for pleasure, but little for Jesus;
  Time for the world with its troubles and toys;
 No time for Jesus' work, feeding the hungry,
  Lifting lost souls to eternity's joys.
 Perishing! Perishing! hark how they call us:
  Bring us your Savior, oh tell us of Him!
 We are so weary, so heavily laden,
  And with long weeping our eyes have grown dim.

 "He was not willing that any should perish;"
  Am I his follower, and can I live
 Longer at ease with a soul going downward,
  Lost for the lack of the help I might give?
 Perishing! Perishing! Thou wast not willing;
  Master, forgive, and inspire us anew;
 Banish our worldiness, help us to ever
  Live with eternity's values in view.

CHAPTER XIV

THE DISPENSARY WORK AT LUPWE

Foreign missionary effort is generally divided into the following four classes:

Evangelistic work
Educational work
Medical work
Industrial work

The *evangelistic* is by all means most important. Educational, medical and industrial have their value only in so far as they are built upon a strong evangelistic foundation. They are only means to an end; they are giant helps to strengthen the evangelistic work.

Now it is quite impossible for any one missionary to be qualified for all these separate branches of service. It is, however, exceedingly important that not one of these branches be wholly neglected, and so the pioneer missionary, whether or not qualified to perform a given work, must earnestly endeavor to be "all things to all men."

The ideal way to do mission work is to have a complete staff: (*a*) A fully qualified ordained minister, who will supervise and have charge of all the evangelistic work; (*b*) a teacher who will have complete charge of all the educational work (the training of such a one should be very thorough and complete as the task of the educational worker is to train native teachers and supervise the village schools where these native teachers will eventually be placed); (*c*) a doctor who will devote all his time to "care of the sick and the dying"; (*d*) a builder and agriculturist who will put up and keep in repair all the buildings belonging to the mission, and who will train the people to improve their living and farming conditions. Such a missionary would be an industrial worker.

How many mission stations are there on the foreign field with such a complete staff? Comparatively few. Especially in Africa. Numerous tribes, spread over large areas, and only few laborers causes each station to continually struggle along under the burden of an incomplete staff. This accounts for the fact that we were only two women workers for the past three years at Lupwe station.

Facing the need, knowing assuredly that it was a gigantic task we prayed daily for strength and courage, asking the Lord to work *for* us and *with* us.

In this chapter I want to acquaint you with the work of the dispensary at Lupwe. In the next chapter we will proceed to the educational and industrial work, and then step over to the most important, the evangelistic work.

* * * * * * * *

Both my co-worker and myself had the privilege of receiving a little medical training before going to the field. While we could not boast of an M.D. after our name, nor would we undertake to amputate a limb, or perform an appendicitis operation, there were many sick people that we were able to help.

Infected eyes are very common in places where hygiene and sanitation are unknown. Many of our people also suffer from tropical ulcers. More than half the patients who come to our dispensary are either eye cases or ulcers. And what a blessing it is that we are able to care for them and after a time dismiss them—healed! It is touching to see the little children with eyes full of pus, unable to open them to the light because of the pain, being carried to our compound. And most of them scream with fright if they see the "strange white lady." We gently wash those eyes and put in the medicine. And then we have the joy of seeing them clear up and get perfectly well. The mother smiles and expresses her gratitude, and often brings to us a little present of peanuts or palm oil. Near the compound of this mother is a boy who has a big ulcer on his leg. He sits about all day long looking very unhappy. He covers the ulcer with a green leaf from the tree so that the flies do not torment him too much. So the mother who came with her baby tells this boy about the "white lady" and the medicine, and invites him to come along with her the next morning. Slowly, with the aid of a stick, the boy walks into our compound and takes his place along with the other patients. Upon their first visit we are careful not to use medicine that will be too painful. We must seek to gain their confidence rather than frighten them away. After a few days' treatment, an expression of hope is seen on the little boy's face. Pretty soon he can throw his stick into the bush, as it is no longer needed. And after a few weeks he is healed. I often wonder who is most happy, the boy or the missionary?

So they come—men, women and children. Some days only a few will come. Then again, we have had as many as thirty on a single day.

Alas, some come with diseases that we are not able to treat. Leprosy is to be found in practically every village of this district. There are cases of sleeping sickness. Some come with large tumors, and sometimes the blind come to see if we have medicine to restore their sight. The nearest doctor (a government official) is seventy-five miles from us. Rarely can we persuade anyone to go that distance and seek his help. They are timid and dare not set out to go to some place where they have never been before.

Some patients come to us from many miles away. It is not possible for them to make daily visits to the dispensary, and so we must make provision for them to stay on the compound. We must keep them quite separate from the other folk, the school boys and our personal helpers. So at one end of our compound we built six huts. One of these we use as the dispensary; and the others are used for resident patients. We make it a rule not to take such patients unless some one of their family will come with them to care for them, providing them with food, drinking water and firewood.

Last July I was alone on the station for two weeks. The school-boys were having a month's vacation and had gone to their several homes. My co-worker was at Wukari for a short change and vacation. I walked down to the dispensary to take care of the patients. I looked into the first hut to greet a patient who had been there for about two weeks. I got no response, but the other patients sitting about began to laugh. The light being so bright outside I could not see the man in the hut. I went a bit closer and the man lay dead on the floor. The ants were crawling all over his thin body. I took a skin and covered his body. Then I sent a boy off to the relatives to ask them to come at once. He did have a wife, but that night they had left him alone. The sons came to take the body and bury it. I felt obliged to tell them what a terrible thing it was that they had left their father alone to die—no one to give him a drink of water or to make a fire for him.

Let me tell you of the first patient who died on our compound. I did mean to pass on and not tell you this. But, on second thought, why should you not know by reading the sadder part of life that a missionary must know by seeing and handling?

It was our first year at Lupwe. I was doing all the dispensary work at that time. One afternoon a man came to see me. After the customary greeting, he asked me whether he could bring his wife to our compound for medical treatment.

"Where do you live?" I asked.

"At Lumbu," he said. That is a hill some six to eight miles from us.

"What is the trouble with your wife?"

"She has a very big sore here," pointing to the upper part of his leg.

"How long has she had this sore?"

"While she has had that sore, we have harvested our fields four times." (That meant the sore was four years old.)

"Have you never tried to do anything for it?"

"All that I have is gone. I have given it all to the spirits and begged them to help my wife. Instead of helping, her sore gets bigger and deeper."

"Will your wife be able to come here, so I can see her?"

"My friends will help me to bring her."

"Very well then. You may bring her, and we will see whether we can do anything for her. When will you come with her?"

"After we sleep twice I will bring her." (Day after tomorrow, as we would say.)

He kept to his word. On that appointed day, toward noon, a little black woman was brought into our compound. Part of the way they had carried her. And then she would try to hobble with the help of a strong stick. By the time she reached our place, she was tired and had a good bit of pain. I greeted her, but then let her rest a while. At first she was shy and shook with fear. She had never seen a white person before, and I could tell she was much afraid of me. Before the first week was over, her fear had flown, the horrible ulcer began to look clean, the pain was lessening, and the little lady began to talk to me. One day she said, "I had one baby, then it died. I never again had another baby. And I got this sickness. I guess the spirits are angry with me." We told her of the Lord Jesus, and encouraged her to ask Him to help her. She listened eagerly to the gospel messages. The ulcer was getting better and she was so happy. Then one week end I had to go to Takum. When I left the patient had a cold, and I gave her medicine for this. I went away on Saturday afternoon. Tuesday, after sunset, I came back to Lupwe. Just after supper, one of the boys came running to me, "Hurry, hurry, white lady, the little woman is dying!" Taking a lantern, I rushed to the huts in the rear of the compound, and found the patient about ready to breathe for a last time. Her husband was there. In his way he was trying to prolong life. He took the brass bracelet from her arm and put it between her teeth to open her mouth. He shook her head to make her eyes move. He spoke to her. He lifted one arm and then another, in a vain endeavor to keep her alive. But I saw that all this was useless. Her lips were sealed for good. She would speak no more. I tried, in a tender way, to tell the husband she was dying, and that his effort would not help her. After she was gone, I gave him a message and we there had prayer—the bereaved husband kneeling with the few Christians who were with me, and myself. Then I got a grass mat and laid this over the corpse of my friend. We secured the doorway against the intrusion of a leopard or other animal, and went to rest. I concluded that the patient contracted pneumonia and that this was the cause of her death. That very day she had been seen gathering a little wood for a fire. No doubt a high fever gave her chills. And it was the rainy season.

I went to my hut, but the pitiful sight of the death of this patient followed me. A few sticks from the bush, laid across one another, was her bed. Being thus raised a bit from the clay floor, she would be protected from the damp. The sum total of all her clothing was one bunch of wilted leaves. She had no blanket. Thinking this all over, I sobbed until nearly midnight. We were not to blame, as nobody knew that she was so very sick. What a great deal of misery and suffering there is in this world, and especially where Christ is not known!

The next morning I went back to the hut and found the husband sitting beside the body of his wife, crying and shaking his head. One of our native Christians helped me to lift the corpse and wrap it for burial. Rev. Whitman was seeing to the digging of the grave. Let me whisper to you, kind friend, that only the enabling grace of our compassionate High Priest can help the missionary to bear the strain of these duties.

That was our first funeral at Lupwe.

We asked the husband to stay with us for a time. To work as a laborer on the place and receive instruction in the things of the Lord. We knew that the people on his hill would say that we had killed his wife; or they would decide that her coming to us made the spirits angry and they refused to help her. I freely told him this, and he stayed with us for three months, and is still very friendly, coming often to greet me. I long that he may come to the knowledge of the Savior!

* * * * * * * *

As I told you before it was my privilege to have a year of special maternity training in one of our big New York hospitals before going to Africa. I have found this training to be of great value, as it has permitted me to help all of our Christian women when giving birth to their children. There is no doctor in the

istrict. So many women have died in childbirth, or from com-
dications that arise, due to their ignorance, carelessness and filth.
nd at such a time a woman gets no sympathy whatever. One
unday afternoon I was called to a village two miles away to see
I could help one of the wives of the chief. I found her sitting
n a stone inside the hut. (It is the usual thing for a woman to
it on a stone at such a time.) She was without a covering on
er body. A little fire in the middle of the hut filled the place
ith smoke. Two or three other women were in the hut, and
ey were very harsh to the patient. They slapped her, and
ushed her, and spoke sharply to her, but she responded very
ttle. She was thoroughly exhausted and a trifle unconscious.
he had been in labor six days. I went to the chief and told him
at she would surely die, that he had waited too long to call me.
he next morning I returned and was able to deliver the child,
hich had been dead for some time. The patient was quite
nconscious, and I was certain there was not a ray of hope for
er. I returned home, and at noon a messenger came to tell me
at she had died.

But I have been able to help several other women. All the
bnormalities and complications that arise at such a time are
onsidered to be the patient's fault. By some sin that she has
ommitted, or because she has not brought sufficient sacrifice to
e spirits; they are angry and refuse to help her. That is why
e gets no sympathy, but only harsh treatment. The blind
easoning of the heathen is: "You are only suffering for your
wn sin, therefore suffer!"

How glad the Christians are to have help at such a time. They
re so appreciative, for well do they know the difference. And
hat a privilege for the missionary to be able to show sympathy,
speak a tender word, to minister lovingly in the name of the
reat Physician, in an hour of great need!

To prove this let me quote from a letter I received from one
f the leading Christians in our little flock. Both he and his
ife are baptized Christians. About two weeks after I helped her
ith the birth of their third child, I received the following:

"This little writing comes from the hand of ——, and his wife ——, and goes to our Baturiya. Greetings and love that knows no bounds we are sending you. Baturiya, even up to this time we have not made to you the proper thanksgiving for the help which you have given to us, and we said that it is right for us to do so now. We thank you very much, very much, and very much, until there is no end of thanksgiving. We also thank our Father, Whom we serve, for He is our great Helper. Also, all the help which you have given us, we know that it is for the sake of the Lord. Baturiya, see here is 5s ($1.25) from us to you. If you will agree, please accept it—not for anything, only because of all your help to us. Again we thank you very much and very much. May the fellowship of our Lord Jesus continue to abide among us. Amen."

I have literally translated this from the Hausa language. I called the writer, and told him that I could not accept the money ($1.25 represented a whole week's wages) but that we would put it in the Lord's treasury as a thanksgiving offering to Him from Whom all blessings flow.

* * * * * * * *

Now we have visited our dispensary work. Do you think it is worth while? In ministering to the body, we have a glorious opportunity to bring a gospel message. So the medical work is a means to emphasize the evangelistic, which is most important.

CHAPTER XV

"Teaching them to observe all things whatsoever I have commanded you. . ."

CHAPTER XV

THE BOARDING SCHOOL AT LUPWE

In pioneer work, as I have explained before, it is not wise to gather up so much work on the mission compound (intensive effort) that makes it impossible for the missionary to go about in the district. On the other hand, it is self-evident that we cannot get on very far in missionary work without a school. Just as soon as a school is established the missionary is bound by a strict routine. Bells have to be rung on time, classes organized, work corrected, and many more things, too numerous to mention, must be carried on with due regularity.

At Lupwe, shortly after I returned from my first furlough, I felt led to establish a boarding school. By boarding school we mean that the pupils, attending such a school, would live on the mission compound. The missionary would be responsible to see that the pupils had huts to sleep in; food to eat; covering for their body, etc. In other words the missionary would have sole charge —be the guardian of these pupils. Just why did we start such a school, involving so much work and responsibility? For two reasons:

First—There were some fine young men at Takum who were prepared to make public confession of faith in Jesus Christ. They were ready to say farewell to the spirit worship, the religion of their ancestors, and eager to receive training in the Christian religion. They were not able to read or write. Though we might gladly encourage them to publicly confess Christ, we could not think of giving them the sacrament of baptism. It is a rule in our mission that at least two years must elapse from the time a candidate makes his first public confession to the time he receives baptism. This is a very necessary rule which we heartily endorse. During that time the candidate must receive instruction. He must learn to read the Word of the Lord; cover the first catechism which contains one hundred questions and answers; be able to memorize the Ten Commandments, the Lord's Prayer, and the Apostles' Creed; become familiar with the early history of Genesis; and know the important facts of the life of Christ. Besides this he must have instruction in practical Christianity. Remember that he is a convert from dark paganism. He does not know *when* to pray, *how* to pray or *why* to pray. He does not know the meaning of the Lord's day and how it is to be used. Indeed, all that God requires of us in His Word must be explained to these converts. Now if the convert is married it is not wise to ask him to come to the boarding school. He must abide at home, let his light shine and endeavor to win the other members of his household to Christ. It may take much longer than two years before he can receive the sacrament of baptism, as he

Boarding school pupils, in their Sunday clothes, entertaining a government inspector with a drill. See page 139.

will not have so much time for study. But if the convert be unmarried, we ask him to come for one year to the school at Lupwe. It is amazing how much such a one can learn in a year. To them it means sacrifice, as they receive no financial remuneration, and are obliged to do a good share of outside work. They also have to buy their own books—New Testament, hymn book and catechism. They may be wanting to get a dowry, but this too must be set aside for a year. Several expressed their desire to have such a year of training and this was the first reason for our establishing a boarding school on the mission compound.

Second—As I toured the district, remembering that certain villages could be reached only once or twice in a whole year, I asked myself this question: "When will these people be able to intelligently accept the message of salvation they have never heard before?" They can take in only a little bit of the truth during one visit a year, and they forget so soon. Then the thought came to me that if we could gather some of the boys from different villages, bring them to a boarding school on the mission compound, pray that they might be converted, surely God would call from among them some who would become teachers and evangelists. They could then return to their home town and village and lead their people to a knowledge of the Savior. Here then is our second reason for establishing such a school.

With this end in view—helping converts that they might receive instruction that would fit them for baptism, and training a certain number of youths in the hope that some of them would become teachers and evangelists to their own people—we prayerfully started this boarding school.

Our total enrollment for the two and a half years that we had this school on the station would number between forty and fifty. Some came for one year and then went back to their work. Others could stay only six months. We never kept more than twenty-five at a time. We could have had a larger enrollment, but our time and strength demanded that we keep the number limited to twenty-five.

For a good part of last year we had seven young men who had publicly confessed Christ, and it was a great joy to me to conduct a special Bible class for them. I also gave them catechism instruction outside of school hours. They *came* to us without ever having seen the alphabet; they *left* with a New Testament which they were able to read. When they first came, they sat with closed lips during the singing of the hymns; when they left they possessed a hymn book and could find the place as the number of the hymn would be announced. The mental training, plus the regular life, proper food and sufficient exercise even changed their physical form and facial expression.

What about the other youths? Were we successful in getting the parents' consent for them to go away from home and attend school? Yes, here too the Lord answered prayer. The chief of the town of K——, fifty miles away from our mission station gave me two fine boys. When he saw how well they looked after six months, and how happy they were to be at school, he brought me his little son of four, and said, "Here, white lady, I give you this my boy for a present. He is yours. Take him with you." I said that he was too small to leave his mother, and I also explained to him that I was not wanting children for presents, or as slaves, but only to have for a time to teach them about the Lord Jesus. During a subsequent visit to this town, the chief again approached me about this little boy: "Is my boy big enough now to come to school?" he asked me. I said he would have to wait at least four years. We would rather not take the boys until they are ten years old. In this whole town of K—— there was no one who had ever possessed a book of any kind. And one day the New Testament entered that town, carried by the two lads that had been in our school. And what is more, they were able to read it. The chief asked them to open the book and read to him, and they were able to do this. They also explained to the chief how they learned to pray, and soon they were kneeling and offering prayer, at the request of the chief who wanted to hear his boys pray. Were they sent away from the mission with this New Testament as a gift? No. We never give away any portion of the Word of the Lord as presents. The elder of the two boys came to me one day, expressed his desire to own a New Testament, and asked me if I could give him any work to do in his own time to earn the money. The price of a New Testament is two shillings (50 cents). I gladly gave him work. He went to the bush and cut grass for the roofs of our huts. Then he wove this grass (i.e., tying little bunches together until it looks like a long piece of fringe) and on other days he would draw water. What a happy boy he was when I called him, and said that he had fifty cents saved, and he could have his Testament. I put a paper cover over the binding to keep it clean, and wrote his name inside, and the name of his town. When vacation time came, he gladly carried along this little extra weight to show to his people. Again I ask you the question: "Who do you think was most happy, the boy or the missionaries?"

I could tell you a like story of other boys who have been permitted to come to us from different parts of the district.

Quite naturally the question arises in your mind, "Do you not have any girls in the school?" Considering the condition of the land you will agree with me that we cannot have co-education. That is, we cannot have girls and boys of the same age in one school. Nor can we get girls for our school. They are promised for marriage while very young, and after that time they are carefully guarded. We have not thought it wise to try and convince the people (I refer to the heathen) that it is quite right for them to send their daughters to school as well as their sons. Besides this, we are keen for the boys because they are to be the future leaders. Our Christian parents, however, want their daughters to be taught how to read and write and they ask me to take them into the boarding school. I have consented to take them only at a certain age. They may come when about eight years old, and stay until they are eleven. This is a long enough period for them to get a good start in reading and writing and to have a little arithmetic and sewing. So last year we had three such little girls in our school by special request of a Christian parent. We also had two married girls, wives of two of our Christians who were working at Lupwe, and to these special instruction was given. It would not be practicable to put them in the regular classes.

In our district of eighty miles there was no other school, so we never had to think about competition. We could make our rules and curriculum as we thought best. We decided to give the children a good bit of outdoor work, especially farming. We would expect them to draw all the water necessary for cooking, drinking and washing, as well as gather the firewood. As much as possible the older boys would help with any building of new huts in the dry season. This would be a great help in keeping down expense, and it would keep the pupils occupied. They are not able to concentrate many hours a day on brain work. The first period each morning would be devoted to the Bible (three mornings to Bible history, and two periods to memory work). For the rest of the time they would have the following subjects: reading, writing, arithmetic, drawing, singing, sewing, handwork, drilling and games.

You may be interested to know our daily program.

5:30 A.M.	Rising bell
6:00	Morning worship in the chapel (except Sunday)
6:30 to 8:45	Outside work
9:00	Breakfast
9:20	First school bell
9:30	Roll call and opening exercises
11:00 A.M. to 2 P.M.	Noon rest and dinner (Due to the heat, we have a long noon rest.)
2:00 to 3:30	Afternoon school
3:30 to 5:00	Outside work
5:00 to 6:30	Recreation
6:30	Evening meal
8:30	Bedtime

Catechism classes are held from 4:30 to 5:30 P.M.

From the station of Wukari we obtained a Christian who had received a year of special training as pupil teacher. He was a very great help to us, and was able to carry on with the work whenever the missionary could not be there. His wife also is a fine Christian, and they have three children of their own. It meant a great deal to have this Christian family on our compound. They had the respect of all the pupils, and their Christian

onduct as well as their home life was exemplary in every way.
do sincerely praise God for giving us this help. The name of
his teacher is Filibbus (Philip), and the name of his wife is
stira (Esther). These Bible names were given them when they
eceived the sacrament of baptism.

There is always one great danger connected with a boarding
chool. The pupils love school, they soon sense that there is a
ast difference between the atmosphere of the Christian com-
ound and their native village. They get regular meals at school,
vhile at their native village they often have to be content with
nly beer. Especially is this true when they have days of spirit
vorship and dancing, as is their custom at set times during the
ear. The pupils feel the touch of fair discipline and loving per-
onal interest, which are unknown in a heathen village. Some
f them are not at all happy to go home at vacation time. Last
uly, one little fellow had to be pushed along the path to get
tarted on his homeward journey. They do not object to the
valk. Barefooted they walk anywhere from four to fifty miles
rom the mission station to their village. And at the end of vaca-
ion, they gladly walk the same distance to return to school. Dare
ve permit them to foster a growing dislike for their own village?

Compound of the boarding school pupils. The little boy in the
front is the son of the Christian helper Filibbus. See page 145.

Shall we silently listen to them criticizing the food prepared by th
hands of their own mother? Will we ever tolerate hearing then
laugh at the ignorance of their father or older brothers? No
And again we say No. Or do you think that this is not a seriou
matter? Then I would inform you that it is a problem which
requires very careful thought. Is it not a terrible thing here a
home, after a father makes great sacrifice to give a son or ,
daughter an education, that the child is ashamed of the parent
Education was never meant to bear such sinful fruit as pride
boastfulness, self-exaltation. We have not as yet decided abso
lutely on a remedy for this danger, but I have come to one o
two decisions. Let me explain to you:

Due to lack of staff our boarding school had to be discon
tinued when my co-worker and I left for furlough early in th
year. We also felt it would be good for the children to be hom
a year. Then, when again starting the school, we could some
what change our methods. This was to us a new experience. I
was a great undertaking to start and continue a school of thi
kind. We have made mistakes, but we wish to correct our mis
takes if we again start the school.

From the beginning we have taken no child without the con
sent of the parents or guardian. There has been ample time nov
for these parents and guardians to see the value of education fo
their boys. They are also unquestionably convinced of the fac
that their boys delight to attend school. They do not have to b
driven from home to come to school. They very gladly exchang
the village fireside with that of the mission compound.

Now we intend to ask the parents to pay a little toward th
training of their children. They cannot give us money. The
never have a plentiful supply of ready cash. But when the
harvest their cornfield, we shall ask them to send a certain num
ber of bundles of corn to school to help feed their children. I
this way both the father and son will be benefited. The fathe
will come to value the training his son is receiving. The son i
later years will never be able to say to the father that he receive
his education from the mission. He will ever have to face the fac
that his father helped to give him a training. This should lea

to a sense of gratitude and appreciation on the part of the son toward his father.

Besides this, I would think it very advisable to have two long vacations each year. One vacation should be in the dry season, the other in the wet season. If these boys could be home with their parents for a whole month in the dry season, they could help do the building work. In every village new huts and new roofs are erected each dry season. I do not mean that the old ones are all torn down or discarded. Some are torn down, but with the increase of wives and children, and with some of the sons getting married, there is always a need for more huts. During the wet season the farm work is done, and the boy could then help on the farm. In this way the boy could spend two months of each year helping his father, and eating the food prepared by his mother. He would constantly keep in contact with his village.

Let me be honest enough to say that this would also help the missionary. It is a tremendous strain to be responsible for a large family. One evening I counted not less than eight interruptions in a single hour. I was busy writing on the typewriter. A boy came to the door, "Excuse me, Baturiya, last night I tore my sleeping blanket; please may I have a needle and thread to sew it?" I go and get what he needs, and return to my work. Pretty soon, "Excuse me, Baturiya, please may I buy a copybook to do some writing?" I take his two pennies, get him a little book, and go back to my work. For a few minutes I tap away hard at the keys, and I hear someone crying on the veranda outside the door. I get up, and there stands a sorry-looking little fellow. "Baturiya, I was playing and stumbled. My big toe hit a hard stone." Yes, the toe was bleeding. "Too bad, come along and we will find medicine and bandage in the dispensary." I wash the toe, and put on a white rag, assuring him that it will soon be better. He smiles through his tears, and says, "Thank you." And again I go back to my typewriter. I add a couple of paragraphs to the letter, and another little chap appears, "Excuse me, Baturiya." "Yes, who is there?" "It is G——" "You may come in." He seats himself on the mat and begins to

greet me. After a little pause, I ask him whether he has come
for anything. "I just came to say greetings to you." But soon he
has courage to ask the favor he intended to ask. "Please,
Baturiya, we are asking whether you will agree to let us come
here a little while after supper, and if you will agree to give us
a book to look at?" I pause a minute to think what I intended
to do that evening. "If you come right after supper, you may stay
for about half an hour." It is a great treat to them to come and
look at a book or some pictures or play with the checkers in the
evening by the light of a lantern. With a broad smile and "Thank
you" he hastens away. And I continue my typewriting. Before
I had finished there were still more interruptions.

Now I do not mean to say that every hour of the day is like
that. Nevertheless the interruptions seem to be continuous on the
mission field, and particularly so where there is a boarding
school. So I do not hesitate to say that it is a great relief to the
missionary to have the children go home for a vacation, so that
he or she may have a change in work.

Probably you will object to our sending the pupils back to
their heathen villages. You say that their surroundings in a
heathen village are conducive to everything except Christian
development. That is true. But, do not thousands of boys and
girls have to live in these surroundings every day of the year?
Must our pupils not learn the value of the gospel of Jesus Christ
and its power to help them to overcome temptation? Must they
never be tested to see how much of that power they possess? In
future years, the Lord willing, we expect them to live as teachers
and evangelists in these surroundings; if we shield them today
will they be very strong tomorrow?

Again, may we not expect them to go into the darkness of
their home village and lift up the torch of the gospel message?

Blessed be our Lord, and blessed be His wonderful grace!
Many of our pupils have returned to their villages and stood up to
tell forth the wonderful story of redemption. They have carried
their New Testament into the village. They have sung the hymns
and taught them to their little heathen brothers. They have
bowed their knees in prayer to the True and Only God. The

Bible tells us, "And a little child shall lead them," and I verily believe that some of these pupils will be used of God to lead others to the knowledge of the Savior.

Several of the parents have visited the mission station, to see their sons, to bring me a little present, and to establish a bond of friendship between us. Then we tell these parents how eager we are that they shall come to know the Lord.

Before closing this chapter I would like to explain about the money used to carry on this work. Thus far all the money has come from voluntary gifts. We have never asked the mission board for an appropriation for this work. Most of the gifts have come from Sunday Schools of the Christian Reformed Church. We are indeed grateful to our Lord that He has supplied all our need.

Some people ask whether they can have the name of a boy and become responsible for his support. And it may seem strange when I tell you that I feel obliged to refuse such a request. Let me tell you why:

In the first place it would increase the burden for the missionary. Already we are overburdened with work on the field. Our correspondence is always neglected. Such a supporter expects to receive reports, letters, a photo, etc., of the pupil. The missionary would have to do this correspondence. Should the pupil be dull, or naughty, the missionary may not want to write that fact to the supporter. But, on the other hand, the missionary may feel duty bound to tell all the truth, and the supporter would be apt to misunderstand the whole situation. Dissatisfaction may arise that would grieve the missionary.

Then too, the supporter may want to write a letter direct to the pupil. The missionary would have to translate this. The pupil would go about with his head lifted high saying to the others, "I got a letter from my guardian over in the white lady's country!" The other children would be jealous and feel very hurt.

At Christmas time a supporter would want to send a present to his pupil. The missionary might not see fit to give this present. Someone sent me a football for a young boy, and another person sent me a vanity case for one of the girls. These children never so much as heard about the presents. It is all right for the whole school to have a football, but not for one boy alone to own such a big plaything. One dear woman (not in America) knit several pairs of woolen stockings for the black boys and girls. These were useless as our people go barefooted all their life. You see how there would necessarily be partiality. One boy would get a pencilbox and another a book, a third some handkerchiefs and a fourth a cap.

Do they not get a present at Christmas? Yes, but we treat them all alike. The smaller boys a present not to exceed twenty-five cents, and the older group a gift that does not exceed thirty-five cents.

The very smallest gift is appreciated by them. One day a boy came into chapel with a safety pin fastened in his curly black hair. That safety pin was quite a big present to this boy.

In this land of plenty and luxury we have so much. It is hard for us to understand how the people in Central Africa live without playthings and luxuries. And we must ever be careful not to spoil them, and it is positively wrong to bribe them with material gifts. We must seek to have them value the gospel above any material thing.

So I think it is better for the people at home to contribute to the school as a whole, and to pray for *all* the pupils instead of for just one individual pupil.

We are certain the Lord has blessed this work of the Lupwe school. It has been a great joy to us. We look forward to its further development, praying that God will establish His Word in the heart and life of every pupil.

CHAPTER XVI

"Lord, speak to me, that I may speak
　　In living echoes of Thy tone;
　As Thou hast sought, so let me seek
　　Thy erring children lost and alone.

"Oh, lead me Lord, that I may lead
　　The wandering and the wavering feet;
　Oh, feed me Lord, that I may feed
　　Thy hungering ones with manna sweet.

"Oh, teach me Lord, that I may teach
　　The precious things Thou dost impart,
　And wing my words, that they may reach
　　The hidden depths of many a heart.

"Oh, give Thine own sweet rest to me,
　　That I may speak with soothing power
　A word in season, as from Thee,
　　To weary ones in needful hour.

"Oh, fill me with Thy fullness, Lord,
　　Until my very heart o'erflow
　In kindling thought, and glowing word,
　　Thy love to tell, Thy praise to show.

"Oh, use me, Lord, use even me,
　　Just as Thou wilt, and how, and where;
　Until Thy blessed face I see,
　　Thy rest, Thy joy, Thy glory share."

Frances R. Havergal

CHAPTER XVI

EVANGELISTIC WORK

Down through the ages, from the very dawn of time, God has called, prepared, and sent forth messengers to proclaim His good tidings. The farewell message of our Lord Jesus included the Great Commission to declare in all the world His finished work of redemption.

How do you picture the service of an evangelistic missionary? What is your idea of the messenger who is called to be a "pioneer worker for Christ?" Have you a picture in your mind of the missionary standing comfortably under a shady palm tree—Bible in hand—with a large group of heathen about him who are eagerly drinking in the Truth? When you have finished reading this chapter I hope that picture will have vanished, and that a truer picture will have been set up in its place.

As I have said before the evangelistic work is the foundation of all other missionary effort. It is the most important part of our work. I do not feel in any way capable of setting before you just all that it involves. You will continually bear in mind that we are dealing with pioneer work among a very primitive people.

Here then is a district at least eighty miles from the northern to the southern boundary line. In all that territory there is no European trading store, no resident government official, no school, no hospital, no doctor, but there are thousands of Africans sorely in need of help.

We were the first white missionaries to be stationed here, and were expected to evangelize this entire district. We were intrusted with that sacred task of bringing to these people—living in unspeakable darkness and ignorance—the good tidings of Him who said, "I am the Light of the world."

Our first duty would be to go about in the district as much as possible visiting the people, and telling them the message of salvation. The people live rather scattered, and the country is very hilly, making it necessary for us to go on "trek" often if we are to reach them at all.

You will recognize the word "trek" as a pure Dutch word. It is very commonly used among the missionaries in Africa, no doubt originating with the Boers in South Africa. To go on "trek" means to go camping or touring through the district.

About four months of the year—part of the rainy season—it is quite impossible to go trekking through the district (especially for a woman). The paths are very muddy; many of the bridges are washed away (native-made bridges); one may have to wade through long deep swampy places; the rivers are full—so full sometimes and with such a swift current that the natives are not willing to take one across in a canoe; and very often the mis-

Two Christian natives going through the bush on a preaching tour. The hill in the background is Lissan. See page 153.

sionary gets a poor tumble-down shack to sleep in. Should one get a drenching by night with a heavy rain that has trickled through a thin grass roof, there would be danger of fever or dysentery. But all these difficulties a missionary may try to overcome by carrying a tent along, and other means. There is one outstanding difficulty. The ground is damp and cold. The people for the greater part are without clothes. They refuse to come to a gospel service and sit about shivering with the cold. A tiny hut, with a goodly number of folks to keep each other company, a fire with plenty of smoke, one common friendly pipe to be passed from the lips of one to another—that is happiness for the native during many days of the rainy season.

Then we choose the dry season to do this work of trekking. If there are any huts to be built, or new roofs to be put on, this must be done during the dry season. Such work requires close supervision. The missionary cannot be in two places at once. He is often forced to spend a part of the dry season at home, getting the building work accomplished, even though he would rather be giving all that time to tour the district. But he will always devote a good share of the dry season to direct evangelistic work in the district.

Having made several such treks, I would like to take you along to see some of the places in our district.

We first decide how long a trek we are going to make. That is, how many days we propose to be away. Sometimes I go for five days and nights, sometimes for ten or fifteen days. The longest trek I ever made was twenty-three days.

Having decided how long we intend to be away, we proceed to get the loads ready. Campbed and bedding, chair, folding table, lanterns and kerosene, cooking utensils and dishes, clothes, a few books and writing material, some native food and a box of tinned food (evaporated milk, coffee, tea, sugar, cereal, rice, etc., etc.) all have to be taken along. It may amount to from five to ten leads. For each load we must find a man who will be willing to accompany us on the trek. These men we call "carriers."

These arrangements completed, we start off. Each carrier will tie his own sleeping mat on his load, lift the load (which weighs fifty or sixty pounds) to his head, and "catch the road," as we say in Hausa. I always take along a trustworthy baptized married Christian to act as guide, spokesman, and adviser, as well as to assist in the preaching. Then there will be a personal boy, whose work it is to pack and unpack the loads, build the fire in the open, and do such simple cooking as one requires on trek. So our company may number ten: seven carriers; a Christian to help with the preaching; a personal boy and myself. I patiently wait until I have seen the last of them "catch the road" and then I mount the bicycle and start off.

It is to me a new path. It is the first time I am trekking this part of the district. Our first stop will be nine miles from Takum. The day before I sent word to the chief of the village and he is expecting us. Should I get ahead of the others I wait along the way until the Christian helper and personal boy come along. Having no loads to carry they are able to walk fast. It is not native etiquette for me to go into a town or village unescorted, and it would be very foolish for me to enter a place alone upon a first visit. We turn to the path that leads to the village. The chief seeing us come, immediately makes haste to meet us with a greeting of welcome, and leads us to the place where we are to camp for the night.

Then we greet each other rather profusely.

He begins by saying "welcome! welcome! welcome!" several times in succession.

I respond by repeatedly saying, "Thank you! thank you!"

"Have you come well?" he asks two or three times over.

"I have come well!" I answer each time.

"And is your tiredness well?"

"My tiredness is with ease."

"Have you left all the people at your compound well?"

"They are well, thank you."

Then I begin to respond to his greeting, by asking him several questions, as to his health, his household, his work, etc.

I tell him the purpose of our visit, and ask him whether he is willing to gather his people to hear the message of God. We agree on a definite time that he suggests. Some prefer a meeting before sundown, others prefer it after their evening meal if it is warm and a moonlight evening.

Before he leaves I ask him whether he will kindly send a man to the village where we intend to sleep the next day, so that the chief there may be informed of our coming. In doing Christian work it is well to be considerate, and I have found that it is not good policy ever to enter a village unannounced.

After these preliminary greetings, the chief asks to be excused, and says, "I will send you firewood and water at once, and a little later I will call the people together." I thank him, and he leaves.

Pretty soon the carriers come along, one after another, glad to be relieved of their load. Generally the chief sends a pot of gruel for them to drink. (At first they often brought us native beer, which we felt constrained to refuse after explaining our reason.)

The boy gets busy setting up the camp furniture, and to make a little fire. We missionaries drink a great deal of tea in Africa. Fresh hot tea, not too strong, seems to quench thirst more than anything else. Consequently, after every journey, the first order on the program is "a kettle of boiling water to make a pot of tea."

You may ask what kind of a place they give the missionary to sleep in. Sometimes it is a very good hut, a little bit away from the village. Then again it is a hut in the compound of the chief, where you will have plenty of visitors—women and children, but also goats, sheep and fowls. It has often been nothing more than a roof set up on eight or ten poles that were planted in the ground. This is very hot, gives one no privacy whatever, and is a good invitation to any animals that may prowl around by night. I shall not soon forget one sleeping hut that was specially built for me when the people heard of my coming. They had never seen a white woman before. No doubt they were frightened. Right in the bush, a long way from the village, they had hastily erected a cute little grass shack. I would have had to crawl in, and there was not space enough for a campbed. The Christian helper said, "You will not sleep here in the bush, Baturiya; I have a friend in this place, and will go and see if he will give you one of his huts." This he did, and I slept in the village. I should not doubt if some of the people did not sleep that night, for fear of my "spirit." To meet this uncertainty about a suitable place to sleep, I have decided to take a strong tent with me the next time I return to the field, the Lord willing.

After we all have a little rest, at the set time we go to the chief's compound, where the people will be gathered. Generally there is a large space, cleared and swept, where the people can sit on the ground around their chief whenever he has a palaver with them.

We greet the chief and the people, explain the purpose of our gathering, and then endeavor to make plain to them the way of salvation. Where and how shall we begin? "For God so loved the world . . ." But they do not know who God is. Try this: "All have sinned, and . . ." They do not know what sin is and where it came from. I once pleaded with an old chief who was dying, "Repent and believe!" He said, "Repent of what? I have never done any wrong. I never stole another man's wife, and I never killed anyone with the 'poison cup.' There is nothing for which I need repent." So this man had lived years, and was about to die, with the false notion that there were only two sins which it is possible for anyone to commit. How would it be to say, "Do you see this Book (holding before them the Scriptures)? This Book tells us a wonderful story . . ." That would be far too abstract. What does a book mean to a group of heathen who are seeing it for the first time. What a privilege it is to bring the gospel! Yes, indeed, but what wisdom is required to know how to present that gospel!

It is necessary, first of all, that we present the message in a very simple manner, in order that all may understand and follow our words. Then, so that it may be fastened upon their mind, we must repeat and repeat the same thing over, asking questions as well.

I have found it well to teach them that God is a Great Personal Being who sees us, but we cannot see Him; the giving, sustaining, and taking away of our lives is in His hand; man plants the corn, God gives the sunshine and rain so that man may be permitted to harvest. To enlarge upon these great truths, I point to their fields and explain the matter carefully. Then I point to a baby in the arms of a mother and say that God has granted that little life; the parents do not know how long they will hold that child in their arms, but God knows. Then I tell them that God made two people, and that we all come from those first parents. "My skin is different from yours, but my blood is just the same as yours," I say to them, and at once I have a strong hold upon their attention. Then I tell them how God put before Adam and Eve two roads—the path of *obedience* and the path of *disobedience;* and all that would result if they chose the path of disobedience. Then I tell them that Adam listened to the voice of the Devil and today we have sickness, hunger, weariness, sorrow and death, all over the world as a result of sin. Then I proceed to acquaint them with Christ—Who came to save us from our sin.

Upon a subsequent visit I will question them carefully to see what they remember. Very often they will remember the names of Adam and Eve, and remember the name of Jesus and that He is the Son of God.

On rare occasions I have seen people weep as they were hearing for the first time the story of the death of our Lord. They very often gasp with wonder and clap their hands in gratitude to God for His gifts as I explain them one by one. And they make expressions of pity and sympathy as I tell of how they nailed the Righteous One to the cruel cross. In this way the missionary is often interrupted during the message, but such interruptions are to be welcomed and never silenced.

It is very unwise to present to the people a one-sided truth. I mean to tell them only of a God of love. They are constantly in bondage of fear because of the spirits, and a God of love does not make a strong appeal. They are far more attracted to such truths as the power and greatness of God, the absolute justice of Jehovah and His wrath toward sin. The story of the flood—

God punishing the sinner—makes a tremendous appeal to these primitive peoples.

After our meeting, we bid the people good-bye, and when we leave the village we ask them to bring us a "return visit" if possible.

The next morning at dawn we have all the loads packed and after a word of prayer together, we start off for our next village.

It would be nice to stop two or three days in each place, but this is not possible. I have often wished to stop in one of the larger towns for a month, holding daily meetings, visiting every compound, and also going to all the nearby villages with repeated visits, but due to the fact that we have such a small staff it is not possible to be away from the station for too long a time. Being only two women, it means that we are both alone; while one is trekking through the district, the other is alone "keeping the homefires burning," the compound school and dispensary.

Pa'ana, "The Daughter of Prayer." (First woman baptized in the Takum district.) See page 179.

At last, after about eight days, we come to the far-off boundary of our district. We are fifty miles away from home. Here is a broad river to cross. The same river in which the two missionaries were killed by the hippopotamus. The town is on the other side of the river. I sit down under a shady tree to wait for some of my company to come along and step with me in the canoe. I dare not enter this town alone, as it is my first visit. It is getting toward noon, and the sun is so hot. I hear voices, and soon see the smiling faces of the Christian helper and my personal boy. One of them runs down to the edge of the water and calls over for the people to come with the canoe— "the white lady is waiting here."

After about twenty minutes the canoe arrives. Two men and a small boy form the crew of the canoe. The two men do the paddling, using short home-made paddles that splash their way through the water. The little boy sits dipping the water out of the canoe. It has a leak in the bottom, and the boy keeps on dipping the water out just as fast as it oozes in. I am asked to step in and find my place. I generally kneel on the flat bottom of the boat and hold onto the sides with my hands. This is most comfortable and if there is water, one does not get too wet. Then my wheel is brought in and laid across the sides of the canoe. Then the two others of my party step in. A good push sets us off. It is a heavy load for a tiny boat, and the sides are down in the water up to an inch from the top. This is by no means a joy-ride. I sit quietly and pray all the way over, and am so thankful when we step out on the other side. At some places they have large heavy canoes, dug out of monstrous trees, but in these little bush towns one generally finds a rickety little ferry.

As we step out on the other side, the drums begin to beat, and a great crowd of people are standing to greet the first white lady who ever entered their village. Their chief is there in "full dress" together with the big men of his town. They escort me to the place where we are to camp. And then we go through the long greeting palaver. They see that I am very tired and hot, as it is between twelve and one o'clock noon, and bid me good-bye after we have arranged about a meeting in the evening.

"Welcome, welcome," I call out to the first carrier who arrives. He has the chair on his load, and so I can sit down. He has the box with the tea, and so I can soon have a hot drink.

They have to wait their turn to be ferried across the river, and so it is a long time before the last one arrives. And they are so hot and tired and thirsty.

Before the kettle boils, I hear some screaming and rough noise. Putting on my helmet I rush out to see that about four of my party are having a first-rate fight. All self-control gone, they are kicking, punching, scratching one another while pouring forth loud speech to show their bitter anger. Soon the others would begin to take sides, and we would have "war in the camp." I took one of the fighters by the back of the neck and pushed him into my own hut. With a second I did likewise, and then commanded the other two to follow. I bade them sit on the floor, each one apart from the other, and not to open their mouth until I gave them permission to speak. At such a time one must be master of the situation, fearlessly proving to possess the superior position. I sat quietly—trembling within, I admit—until the tea was brought, and then took my time to drink it. Meanwhile I was asking the Lord for strength and guidance and for victory over this attack of the enemy. I knew the enemy was on our trail. He will not silently look on while we enter his territory and seek to release men and women from his bondage. I have experienced several battles with this greatest of all foes—the Devil.

For a whole hour the four fighters sat silent. This gave them ample time to cool down a little. One was wounded in the neck, and blood was showing on his black skin.

In a quiet firm tone of voice I started to speak to them, explaining the purpose of our coming to this village, and of how they had yielded to the attacks of the enemy who was always ready to frustrate our efforts. I asked them whether they were willing to confess to one another and forgive. I told them that unless they promised me to continue our stay here, and finish the trek without another such display, I would have the loads packed and we would leave that town at once. I said to them very earnestly, "One of you four is a Christian. All this anger and battle has arisen over a single ear of corn. We have come here to tell the people of Jesus and His peace, but you have exemplified hatred and permitted the Devil to glory in his victory over you. Now choose whether you wish to continue your fight or forgive and settle down to good behavior." I addressed the Christian first and said, "Tell me, N——, what is your choice?" He looked ashamed and said he was sorry to have given in to the enemy, and was very ready to ask the others to forgive him. Two of the others were also ready to take this same stand. The fourth one was stubborn, and not so ready to decide. The victory being so near, I said to him, "Three are willing to forgive, if you are not ready to do the same, you may take your sleeping mat and leave the town to return home. I refuse to have you accompany me further unless you promise to behave yourself." He decided to stay with us. They each acknowledged their wrong, said they were sorry, and promised not to let such a thing happen again. I then told them that unless God worked repentance in us we could not be truly sorry; unless we asked His help our promises were useless; and that we needed to seek His forgiveness. We had prayer together, and I excused them. They kept their promise and behaved well the rest of the trek.

Toward sundown the chief sent a plentiful supply of food for all my party, and they spread out their mats on the ground, seating themselves around the dishes of cornmeal porridge and gravy. Their leader (the Christian helper—who had no part in the fight) said grace; and first put his hand in the dish. They eat with their fingers, but only one dips at a time. They take a little lump of porridge, roll it between their fingers, and dip it into the other dish of gravy or soup. No one will put forth his hand for a second dip until each one has had a first turn. When one is satisfied he will say, "I have finished," and draws back, while the others continue to eat. The married men generally eat in one group, while the single ones form a second little circle, and younger boys have their portion all to themselves in a separate company.

After this we went to the chief's place, and had our meeting. Somewhere around one hundred and thirty men sat before me on the ground. I asked the chief whether he would not call the women, as the message was also for them. He said, "After we hear it, we will tell our women." So we went on with our service, and had a wonderful response. A few women dared to peep around the corner of the grass matting that fences off one compound from another, but none dared to walk anywhere near the group of men. The next day I remained in this village to rest and have another meeting. I sent to the chief to ask whether I might take a stroll through the village and see his town. He sent word back: "The white lady is tired. She has come a long way. It is better for her to rest." It was a verbal message, and I said to the helper who brought the word: "Must I understand that he does not want me to see his town?" He truthfully replied: "You must have much patience with our people, they are afraid because you are new to them. They think if you walk around you may anger the spirits. But they will learn after a while." I contented myself to stay away from the people during the entire visit, except while we had the meetings. The huts where we camped were a little way off from the village, and after each meeting the chief would accompany me to our camping place. He was friendly, kind and much interested.

Today in that village are the two boys whom I mentioned before. They have with them a New Testament and a hymn book. They are able to read and sing. The chief has promised me his son of about five years old. And upon my last two visits to this town the women were present at the meetings. What a marked advance! They formed a large group on one side of me, while the men gathered and seated themselves on the other side. They answered correctly many questions as I reviewed a little of our message. They asked me several questions also. They asked me to come and stay with them in their village, to conduct school, and keep on teaching them. I long for the day when one of these two boys, receiving training at our boarding school, may be stationed as teacher-evangelist in this village! Pray that it may be so!

You will agree with me that it is worthwhile to do this kind of evangelistic work. The hardships of crossing bridgeless streams, crawling over a swinging hammock bridge that shakes with every move one makes, or creeping on all fours over a single tree-log that is placed over a stream as a bridge substitute, or crossing the rivers in a little dugout, are soon forgotten when the joy that knows no measure floods one's soul; the joy of seeing definite results, which will eventually lead to a realization of our prime purpose—Jesus crowned as Savior and Lord in the hearts of these people.

Let me be fair enough to tell you that sometimes we have a very discouraging time. I took one trek through the hills, walking from place to place for nine days. The bicycle is of little use among the mountains. It was the beginning of the rainy season. We planned to stay over Sunday at a certain village, but it proved that we were not welcome. They did not want to provide food for the carriers and the others who were with me. So they suffered a good deal of hunger. Rain hindered the people coming to meetings. I sat at a hut door, with an umbrella to keep me dry, while the people were huddled together inside the hut about a fire. On Sunday afternoon a heavy thunderstorm arose. The rain came down in torrents. The hut where I camped was a grass-walled one, and the rain came rushing in until the whole place was flooded. I sat on a chair with my feet on a big stone, while campbed, table, boxes, etc., were surrounded with the water. For three hours the thunderbolts crashed about us while the lightning lighted up all the bush around. We could have no meeting. After the water soaked in, I had a little supper and went to bed. Early the next morning we started off for a long walk to another hill. Here we found but few people home. They had gone to their farms, which were several miles away from the hill. The chief was at home, but he was sick. We stopped here one night, and decided to go home. How glad we were to see our Lupwe compound. I greeted my co-worker with "Be it ever so humble, there's no place like home." The texts on the wall of our hut spoke a message of hope and encouragement to my soul.

After working for a time, we find that there are those who are ready to stand up and make a public confession of their desire to follow Jesus Christ. They promise to separate themselves from all forms of spirit worship; from all dances connected with such worship; from the use of idols and charms; from all food that has been sacrificed to the spirits or to the dead. They promise to abstain from any drink that has power to make a person drunk. They declare their faith in Jesus as a personal Savior, as the *only* Savior, and that all other religions are false. They agree to submit themselves, if necessary, to discipline, and to put forth every effort to learn such things as are necessary for their growth and prosperity in the Christian life.

They are as yet unable to read the Word, and it is not right to administer the sacrament of baptism immediately upon a first profession of faith in Christ. In chapter XV, I explained what is required of the converts. As soon as a person takes a public stand for Christ he becomes what we call an inquirer. He is called a "follower of the Lord"; is under instruction and subject to discipline. After some time has elapsed and the inquirer proves to be diligent, faithful, and desirous to go forward in his Christian life, he is placed under definite instruction preparatory to receiving the sacrament of baptism. We might call this the second stage, and he is now called a catechumen. He remains a catechumen until such time as he receives holy baptism.

Of course it is the duty of the missionary to provide the necessary instruction for the converts. And so we build a chapel where they can be gathered to receive the help they need. Having a chapel (which may also be used as a school building in the beginning of a work), we decide to have regular services and classes. We built two such chapels, one at Lupwe, and the other at Takum, four miles away from Lupwe. We provided the following services for the converts:

Daily morning worship at 6 a.m. (except Sunday) at Lupwe
Sunday morning worship at Lupwe and Takum
Sunday school (afternoon) at Lupwe and Takum
Prayer meeting (Thursday morning) at Takum
Catechism classes at Lupwe and Takum

You will notice that I have not mentioned the regular day school, because that belongs more specifically to the educational work, and has been dealt with in the preceding chapter.

The missionaries alone can be responsible to decide who of the catechumens shall be first to receive baptism when there are as yet no church members. After baptizing three or four, these baptized members are always consulted before any others receive the sacrament. Thus far we have baptized seven converts. Three others, who have received the sacrament at some other mission station, have come to make their home in Takum, and are thus united to our flock. So we have ten who are eligible to partake of the second sacrament—the Lord's Supper. We try to have communion twice a year. It is necessary to get an ordained minister from one of our other stations to come to us for the week-end and perform such special services as baptism and communion.

There are at least twenty more who belong to the Christian flock, but who are as yet in the catechumen and inquirer groups.

What about the little children born to the believers? Do they receive baptism? No, not as yet. For two reasons. First, we have not had opportunity to teach the converts the doctrine of the Covenant in such a way that they would understand the significance of infant baptism. In part this is due to the fact that we do not have the entire Old Testament translated into the Hausa language. A second reason is tribal custom. It often happens that the parents do not own their children, they are the property of the mother-in-law. All about us is the offensive practice that parents do not bring up their own family. A child of four is exchanged with another child belonging to some relative or friend. It is believed that a child will be spoiled if brought up by its own parents. It often happens that one parent is converted while the other continues in heathendom. Say a father is converted. His wife is a heathen. They have a child. The wife may take that child and give it to her heathen relatives to bring up. The father could not go to the native chief and claim control of his child. This is a native custom which we abhor, but which, at the present time, we stand helpless to overthrow. However, we do not wish to have the children of Christian parents grow up without any recognition in the church. Hence, for the present we have dedication of infants. The parents thereby declare their gratitude to God for the gift of a child, and promise to bring up their own children (not exchange them with the children of un-Christian relatives) in the fear and admonition of the Lord. (In case only one parent is a Christian, he is asked to promise that he will do all in his power to keep the child home, and to teach it the way of the Lord.) The child is given a name, and reckoned with the flock of the believers. In a separate chapter we will tell a little more about the children.

So after five years of evangelistic work in this particular district, the missionary has the joy of meeting a little flock of believers, composed of: (a) baptized Christians; (b) catechumens; (c) inquirers; (d) children of the believing parents.

Have we an organized church? No, not as yet. We do not propose to organize a church in our district until there are at least twenty-five baptized Christians. Our mission has for its ideal a SELF-SUPPORTING, SELF-GOVERNING, and SELF-PROPAGATING African Church. We are seeking to reach this ideal in the following manner:

1. In the hope of establishing a self-supporting church, we urge upon our Christians the duty of tithing. They are asked to tithe strictly of any money they earn, and also to tithe the first-fruits of their farm products. Are you surprised to hear that we have the "envelope system" away out there in this pioneer station? We started it the first Sunday I was on the field after returning from my first furlough. A few are slack and unfaithful, and need to be reminded of their obligation. But the majority are regular and give with pleasure and a cheerful spirit as unto the Lord. Very often farm products—the first fruits—are brought to the home of the missionaries. It is exchanged with money. The food is used for the boarding school, but the money is put into the Lord's treasury. (At Christmas time we ask a special thank-offering of our Christians, and some have given as much as twenty-five cents. This is a large gift when one considers that the average man is unable to earn more than fifty or sixty cents a week. Sometimes a Christian couple will feel constrained to

bring a special offering of thanksgiving upon the birth of a child.) With these tithes we are supporting Filibbus, the only paid worker in our district. The money is not quite sufficient for his entire allowance (he is teacher in the boarding school), but as the number of believers increases the gifts will also increase.

2. In the matter of self-government we have made a good beginning. Three of our best Christians—married men—who, since they reached baptism, have not at any time been put under discipline, have been installed as elders. I insisted upon this as soon as I knew that we two women were to be the only workers in the district. They were installed at a regular Sunday morning service by an ordained missionary. With these three elders we consult in all matters of discipline and government, and frequently charge them with special duties in the little flock, thus teaching them what it is to have oversight of the church of Jesus Christ. For instance, if a catechumen asks for baptism, I will first ask the elders whether they agree, and after they agree, we ask the other church members to give their consent. In the matter of "rules and regulations," it is well not to have the Christians think that the white people are making church laws and demanding their enforcement. Take the matter of drinking beer. The missionaries are not agreed among themselves about this. Some think we should have a rule demanding total abstinence, while others declare we have no such right, that Scripture does not permit us to take away a person's liberty. This is a very serious matter in Africa, where drinking is such a curse. I had a special meeting of the male church members to talk some of these things over. I asked them what was their desire in the matter of converts being allowed to partake of strong drink. Immediately one said, "White Lady, we black people do not know moderation, we do not know self-control. We may say it is all right to drink a little bit, but a black man does not know the difference between a little bit and a whole lot. We will surely have drunkenness. I say with all my heart we must have a strict rule that we make a person abstain from all strong drink." The others all agreed that this was right, and that they wished their

church to have this rule—total abstinence. So we have prohibition—not by the advice of the missionary, but by the common consent and demand of the Christians who are gradually taking the responsibility of self-government.

3. Just what do we mean by a self-propagating church? Every convert must witness to the truth as it is in Christ Jesus. Every believer must be a missionary to tell others of the Christ he has learned to love and serve. The Christians must be asked to volunteer to go to neighboring villages to preach to the people. They must be encouraged to give a part of their time to definite evangelization work. No teachers and evangelists must be employed and supported with home funds. We must establish out-stations in the district and ask the Christians to go and take charge of these out-stations, holding services and helping the people to a knowledge of Christ. And such Christians must be voluntary workers. If they receive any remuneration it must be from the native church, and not from funds received through the mission board. This is very hard. It is so much easier to employ a staff of teachers and evangelists, set them out in the district, and trust them to do their whole duty. But the easiest way is not always the surest. I believe that in a work such as ours, and among a primitive people, we must adhere strictly to the ideal of a self-propagating church. Already we have a beginning, as I hope to explain more fully in a chapter that will be devoted to the story of our first Dzompere convert who became the first voluntary worker in the district.

As soon as out-stations are established the missionary will have to make repeated visits to such places to help and encourage the worker, and to carefully examine the progress of the work.

When a person shows a decided interest in the message of salvation, and requests to be further instructed, the missionary is expected to help such a one. I refer specially to the results of trekking. We have a woman in one village thirty miles away, who is showing a keen interest in the things of the Lord and who has a deep desire to be taught. It is hard to make trips to a village so far away. Nor can we send one of our elders. It will not do for a man to give individual instructions to the wife of another. Nor can we ask the woman to come to our place. Her husband would not give her this permission knowing full well that she would be subject to fierce temptation. Nevertheless, our evangelistic effort must include some way of reaching those who are being drawn by the Spirit of the Lord.

There are many problems that arise. I think it best to deal with a few of these in a separate chapter. But they belong to the evangelistic work, and you will then see how tremendous is the task that confronts the pioneer missionary.

At the present time we are laying the foundation of the Church of Jesus Christ. If the structure is to be permanent, the foundation must be strong and carefully planned. If the foundation is of sand, the structure will be thrown over with the first wind. Persecution is almost sure to arise sooner or later! The enemy will hurl his attacks against the church! May the Lord help us to build upon the rock. May we be supplied with wisdom from above to teach pure doctrines. May discipline be administered in the spirit of Christ. Then God's Spirit will not be grieved, and His striving in the church will not be quenched. O, that our Sender may look down upon the little flock of believers in this Takum district, and declare:

"Fear not, I am with thee, O be not dismayed!
For I am thy God, and will still give thee aid;
I'll strengthen thee, help thee, and cause thee to stand,
Upheld by My righteous, omnipotent hand."

Takum women going to the hill for palm wine.
See page 104.

CHAPTER XVII

"*Coming, coming, yes they are,*
Coming, coming, from afar,
From the wild and scorching desert,
Afric's sons of colour deep;
Jesus' love has drawn and won them,
At His cross they bow and weep."

CHAPTER XVII

FIRST FRUITS

One may be able to fill a single volume with the detailed life story of each one of the converts. I feel constrained to mention only a limited number. When our Lord was upon earth, there were many converts of whom we have never heard even their names mentioned in the Bible. Of the chosen twelve disciples we know very little about their conversion and Christian life. The names of several of them are not even mentioned after the Day of Pentecost.

Our work in this Takum district is so new that I hesitate to speak too glaringly of the results. The work is not yet sufficiently established to know whether each one who makes a profession is truly sincere. From time to time we cross off the name of an inquirer—the path of Jesus Christ being too narrow for them. And it may be that, should tribulation or persecution arise because of the Word, many would be offended.

In the homeland we cannot understand what fierce temptations beset our Christians. On every side of them is polygamy, gross immorality, beer drinking, and immoral dances. Takum has a large native market. This draws great numbers of men from neighboring tribes who pass through on their way to different trading centers. As a result we have in Takum a host of immoral women. Such women are very brazen and dare to approach anyone with an invitation to enter their tents of wickedness. These are the women who go to the hill for palm wine which they get for the price of sin, and take it back to the Takum market to sell to such who are waiting for the palm wine and also for the palm-wine women. On their way to the hill these women have to pass our compound, and frequently they come in, having

for an excuse a request for a drink of water, or for a little fir
to light their pipe.

There is also a great temptation before our Christians whe
their heathen relatives ask them to partake of food that has bee
sacrificed to the spirits.

The missionary spends hours in patient dealing with this on
and that one who has been lured aside into the path of the enem
Out here in Africa, dealing with a child-like people, some c
whom are crawling out of the thick night of heathenism, an
seeking to stand in the light of the Savior, we realize th
force of the Evening Hymn:

> "For some are sick and some are sad,
> And some such grievous passions tear;
> And some have never loved Christ well,
> And some have lost the love they had."

Surely the Apostle Paul lived through these very same exper
ences. Read his epistles, and see how he was continually rebu
ing and admonishing those early Christians. Carnality, fornic
tion, hatred and drunkenness were all there in the church
Corinth. And surely the Devil is not less busy in these days tha
he was in that time. We, the missionaries of the cross, ha
entered the Devil's territory. For centuries he has been holdi
these people in terrible bondage. And now we come to distu
his right-of-way. We come in the name of our Christ, and, whi
Satan may know that already he is defeated, nevertheless in the
days he seems to be working night and day to dethrone the Lo
Jesus in the hearts of men and women everywhere.

But blessed be our God—most of our converts who do yie
to temptation and commit some flagrant sin, come again wi
true repentance, public confession, and the request to be restore

Again I say, blessed be our God, there are those who ha
not turned to the right nor to the left, but who have kept the
eyes fixed upon Calvary, and who have stood, clad in the whe
armor of God, against every onslaught of the enemy. Pray th
they may continue to stand!

Let me first introduce you to the three elders in our lit
flock. I will mention them by their Christian names, i.e., t

names they received at baptism. We do not encourage them to change their names, but sometimes a person has a slave name or a name connected with the spirit worship, and wishes to drop that for a Bible name. Others prefer having two names, retaining the name given them by their parents, and adding a Bible name.

The three elders are Filibbus (Philip), Istifanus (Stephen), Danyelu (Daniel).

Filibbus came to us from Wukari, where he was converted and baptized. He is the one who also helps us as teacher in the boarding school, and who is almost entirely supported by the contributions of the native church. His wife is also a baptized Christian—from the Freed Slaves' Home at Wukari. Her name is Astira (Esther). She was captured when very young or sold to pay off a debt, and thus became a slave. The government found it out, released her, and put her in the home which our mission had for such freed slaves. Filibbus and Astira were baptized on the same day, though at that time there was no thought of their marrying each other. From the beginning he was promising, and the missionaries gave him special instruction in the hope that he would become a teacher-evangelist. He then asked for Astira to be his wife, and it was they who were married shortly after I arrived in Africa. It was the first Christian wedding I saw, and it made a profound impression upon me, to think that these who formerly were heathen, had made such progress in the way of the Lord, as now to be standing in the chapel, before an ordained missionary, being joined together with the Christian marriage ceremony. Little did I think that I would have so much joy with this Christian couple in my work in Africa. The Lord has blessed them with three lovely children, strong, healthy, affectionate little tots. It requires no effort to love them. Filibbus and Astira are very happy. There is so much quarreling between husbands and wives in Africa, that it is a joy when one sees a couple so happy in the Lord, and so truly united. Never do we hear a word of complaint or an uproar. For this year, while the boarding school is closed, Filibbus is stationed at Takum, to help the Christians there. Next year, when I return, the Lord willing, I would like to send him to one

of our other stations for another year of definite training to fur
ther equip him for Christian service.

I do not know of a name in the Bible more suitable to the
character of the second elder, than the name he has chosen, Istif
anus (Stephen). His countenance expresses the peace and joy
that floods his soul. His prayers are in the power of the Holy
Spirit. He is never ashamed of his Lord! He has been used of
God to win four others of his relatives to the Savior. Three
have made public confession at Takum, and the fourth is a
brother with two wives, who is seeking to arrange his matri
monial difficulty before taking a public stand. But I have every
reason to believe that he is sincere, and that he will soon come
into the little flock of believers. Istifanus has one great sorrow
His wife is not a Christian. He has come to me over and over
to pour out his heart about this matter. One day he said to me
"We have been married over eight years. I have never once
quarreled with my wife. We are very happy. I love her. But
she does not love my Lord! I keep on talking to her, praying
with her, and praying for her, and it seems I am waiting so long."
He was very grieved, and I tried to encourage him to continue
in prayer with her and for her. She does sometimes come to
service, and when I left Takum, she walked along the road to
see us off.

> "Savior, Savior, hear my humble cry,
> While on others Thou art calling,
> Do not pass her by."

Istifanus will not permit her to grind corn for beer or making
any food that is to go to the spirit places. Her parents are
heathen, and they have threatened to disown her should she
become a Christian. She is afraid of their threats. They have
begged her to leave her husband, but she clings to him. This
gives us hope that God, in His own time, will reveal to her her
need of a Savior. Istifanus is a resident of Takum and belongs
to the Jukun tribe. He is faithful in attending all services, and
in matters of discipline he is a great help to the missionary. He
is honest to speak his convictions, stern in his attitude toward
sin, but sympathetic in his dealing with the sinner. His own

Christian walk is so honorable that none can ever point the finger to him, and sneeringly remark, "There is a beam in thine own eye!" I do sincerely hope that this elder may be spared for many years, and kept by the power of God, leading many souls to Jesus Christ.

The third elder Danyelu (Daniel) is the first convert from among the Dzompere tribe, and I thought it might be helpful and encouraging if I gave his story in full, and will endeavor to do so in the next chapter.

Having acquainted you with the leaders in the little flock, it is only right that I should next introduce you to the oldest member. Her name is Pa'ana, and I would judge her to be well over fifty years of age. She is a resident of Takum, also belonging to the Jukun tribe. I believe that the bondage of slavery has been her portion for many years. She is a widow, and works for her living, making native food and selling it in the market. She was first told about the Lord Jesus by an inquirer who was led to witness to her about the truth. She came fearlessly to chapel and it was not long before the Savior had entered the open door into her heart. She begged to be baptized. At first the missionaries thought best to wait. Pa'ana could not read, she was poor and needed most of her time to earn a living. She asked one or two of the other women to help her, but they soon lost patience with Pa'ana's poor brain power to retain the letters of the alphabet. Probably her eyesight was not too good either. But at every service, at prayer meeting, at any special class, she was always present. There was no room to doubt her sincerity. And she kept on pleading for baptism. At last we could not put her off any longer. It seemed unfair and mean to hinder her entering the fellowship of the inner circle of believers. So she was baptized. What a happy day that was for her! With devout reverence she partakes of the Lord's Supper! With tears she prays in the prayer meeting, pleading for sinners and for inquirers who are cold or who have gone into sin. She has suffered much in the way of bitter nagging in the market place. She has been pushed out of one place and another, forbidden to sit where she chose to sell her wares. One day I catechized her carefully to

see whether she really understood about the Lord. I was amazed
Though she could not learn to read, surely the Holy Spirit wa
teaching her the things of Christ. She understood thoroughly al
about the birth, life, death, resurrection and ascension of ou
Lord. Also about the future life. With radiant hope she wa
assured of a place in the "City of Gold," in that day when H
comes to "make up His jewels."

She is faithful in presenting her tithe offering unto the Lor
each week. Her envelope is never missing. One Christmas sh
brought a sheep to give as her special thanksgiving offering
Several of the Christians brought native foodstuffs. We distrib
uted these among the blind, the lepers, the aged, the poor o
Takum. The tears came to my eyes as one led the sheep, tie
to a cord, to where we stood. Pa'ana would have to save a lon
time to be able to buy a sheep. But she realized that the wealt
of all eternity was hers now that the Babe of Bethlehem was he
personal Savior.

She is a woman of great prayer, and she seems always to pra
aloud. The other Christians often hear her in her little hu
praying aloud unto the Lord. They have given her this name
"The Daughter of Prayer." Pa'ana did not take a Bible nam
when she was baptized. But surely she could have no mor
beautiful name than the one by which she is always called, no
by her own choice, but conferred upon her by the other believ
ers—The Daughter of Prayer.

Just before my co-worker and I came away from the distric
Pa'ana came to me and asked to buy a New Testament. I sai
to her: "But Pa'ana, what good will the book be to you, seein
you cannot read it?" She said: "I know I cannot read it. No
in this world. But now you and the other lady are going away
We shall be lonesome. I want you to know that I have a Nev
Testament. I shall have it in my hut to look at. I shall hold i
in my hand, and carry it to chapel on Sunday." And she hande
me fifty cents to pay for the New Testament.

Pa'ana cried very bitterly when we left. In silence, togethe
with the other Christians, she walked with us for a long way out
side the town, until I asked them to go no farther, but to retur

ome. Pa'ana broke down and sobbed bitterly. May the Lord
ustain her through this earthly pilgrimage, and when her days
re complete, may He open the gates of heaven to her, saying,
Come in, thou Daughter of Prayer!"

I would like also to acquaint you with one of our other Chris-
an women. Her name is Merimu. She, too, did not take a Bible
ame when baptized. Last November ('25) she received the
acrament and was enrolled with the members in full commun-
n. Rev. C. W. Guinter came to us to perform several special
rvices. Merimu is the wife of a Mohammedan, who is a native
lacksmith, residing in Takum. He is a polygamist. Merimu is
is head wife. She too has had to bear much persecution in her
vn household. Her husband has a violent temper, and all his
her wives run away and leave him after a short time. In a
ngle year he may take several women, but each will run away
ter a quarrel. Merimu, with a patience given to her by the
ord, remains faithful. It is not to be wondered at if she com-
ains about the cruel treatment she often receives, when her
ithfulness and honest character are never appreciated. I
ive spoken to this husband on several occasions, and he has
me to our chapel often. He admits that we teach the truth of
od, but he is not willing to pay the price—live with only
e wife.

It is all of four years ago since Merimu first made public con-
ssion of Christ. And like Pa'ana she is very faithful in church
tendance, etc. Her envelope is never missing on the collection
ate on Sunday morning. She has often gone out with Astira to
sit other women in the town and to tell them of the Lord. She
loved by the people, the heathen as well as the Christians,
cause she is ever willing to help in a time of need. She is
nstantly witnessing to her own relatives about the Lord Jesus.

One of the little girls in our boarding school is the daugh-
r of Merimu. The mother is so anxious that the child shall not
ow up to adhere to the Mohammedan faith, and to be married
a Mohammedan. She wants her to be a Christian, and marry
e of the converts. Merimu also has two married daughters,
d had several husbands herself before she was converted. She

is a woman of about forty-five. May the Great Shepherd of the sheep enable her to endure steadfastly unto the end!

On the same day that Merimu was baptized, a man named Umaru also received this sacrament. He belongs to the Bafum tribe, but has been a resident of Takum for several years. He also made first confession to follow the Lord about four years ago. He was at our boarding school for some months last year. I should judge him to be about thirty years old. He is a splendid Christian, who, as far as we know, has never needed to be disciplined for falling into gross sin.

Last year I was resting for two weeks on one of the high mountains about four miles from Takum. Early one morning we had visitors come to greet us—the brother of Umaru together with a little girl whom I had never seen before. Umaru's brother handed me a note. The note was from the hand of Umaru, and contained a sentence like this: "To my mother, I am sending you for a present this little girl to be your daughter. She is my wife. I have just brought her from my home town far away. Will you please teach her all things she must know to be a good Christian and a good wife?" The little thing was shy and nervous. I asked her: "What is your name?" but she trembled to speak to me. In her hand was a tiny chicken which she was bringing me as a present. I would judge her to be not a day over fourteen. After a little visit with the brother, who is a catechumen, they again went down the mountain to return to Takum. I sent a message and greetings to Umaru the husband. Afterwards he came to our compound with his little girl wife and they both received school training. She is a lovely, bright child and I believe will be a follower of our Lord in all sincerity. I was sad to see her so young and married. But I was also glad to think that she was having a Christian husband, a husband who would not be adding other wives, whereas it might have been her lot to be married to some old man who had a household full of women.

We told Umaru that he would have to stand up with his wife in the chapel and have the Christian ceremony, if he was to be baptized. He was very willing, and so on the same Sunday that he received the sacrament of baptism, they had their marriage solemnized in the presence of God and His congregation. This was a happy day! Some days before, I had asked Umaru whether he wished to take a Bible name, and if so to let me know the name he chose. He said: "I would like the name Matthew." What led him to choose this name? We had been having Bible lessons and I told them about the conversion of Matthew, the feast he made unto Jesus, how the Lord chose him to be a disciple and how later he was honored by the Holy Spirit to write the gospel bearing his name. These lessons made a marked impression upon Umaru. I saw that he was drinking in every word. But I was surprised when he said he wanted to be called "Matthew." He felt that Jesus had called him from the outcast of society just like Matthew, and so he wanted that name. His was baptized "Umaru Matta" (Umaru Matthew). The last message from the field brings me news that a new little life—a baby girl—has come into their home. May their home be a beacon light in the midst of the darkness, and may others be led to Christ through Umaru Matta and his wife, who is now an inquirer.

> "And what shall I more say? For the time
> would fail me to tell of . . . , and of
> . . . , and of . . . ."

Among the group of catechumens and inquirers are others who are very promising. True, some of them need repeatedly to be dealt with because they are lax and unfaithful in their Christian walk, and others have to be crossed off the roll. We took one young man off last year for marrying a second wife. I had warned him, and prayed with him, but he persisted, and then for a long time he stayed away from chapel. But latterly he was again coming to Sunday services. He cannot again be enrolled as inquirer until he puts away the second wife, and makes public confession of his sin.

One woman took it upon herself to make and sell native beer, and she was taken from the roll. But the last Sunday I was in the district we had the joy of seeing her arise with a public confession, and ask to be again restored. She was then again enrolled as inquirer.

Another young man transgressed the seventh commandment, and while he publicly confessed his sin, the elders decided to make him wait two years before receiving baptism.

Still another was tempted to eat food sacrificed to the spirit of a dead man. He was hungry and tired and fell before this temptation. No one saw him eat this food, no one would ever have known it, but the Spirit of the Lord gave this young man no rest until he came to confess his sin.

We very often think of the words of the Great Apostle:

> "We are troubled on every side, yet not distressed; we are perplexed, but not in despair; persecuted, but not forsaken; cast down, but not destroyed."

If, dear friend, you are among that large number who pray continually for the welfare of Zion; for the breaking down of the strongholds of Satan; for the spread of the blessed gospel message, that the peoples who sit in darkness might see the Light, then I have told you enough in this chapter to make you extol with the psalmist,

> "I love the Lord, for He hath heard my voice and my supplication."

CHAPTER XVIII

"God is working His purpose out as year succeeds to year,
 God is working His purpose out and the time is drawing near;
 Nearer and nearer draws the time,
     The time that shall surely be,
 When the earth shall be filled with the glory of God
     As the waters cover the sea.

"All we can do is nothing worth unless God blesses the deed:
 Vainly we hope for the harvest-tide till God gives life to the seed;
 Yet nearer and nearer draws the time,
     The time that shall surely be,
 When the earth shall be full of the glory of God
     As the waters cover the sea."

CHAPTER XVIII

THE FIRST CONVERT FROM AMONG THE DZOMPERE

Tribal customs are very strong among the Dzompere. The women and children live in constant terror. Should a man die and leave two or three wives, these women will not have the privilege to marry whom they please. At once they become the property of the eldest brother of the dead man. This brother may claim the women for his own wives, or he may sell them, or he may exchange them to secure others for himself. In this way a widow, together with her children, become slaves. They have no liberty of their own whatsoever.

In the event of children being left orphans, they also become the property of their father's brother. If there are many children, they may be divided among several brothers, but the older brother will have charge of the dividing, and he may take two or three and give a younger brother only one.

On one of the hills near us a boy and a girl became orphans. They were still quite young. The girl was kept and sold to a man on another hill. The boy was appropriated by the father's brother. It so happened that the big chief visited this hill one day, and asked about this orphan boy. He expressed the desire to have the lad come to his compound. Who would dare to refuse the desire of the big chief? All the people were afraid of him, and all his requests would be immediately granted. Not because one wished to heed his wishes, but because one was afraid of consequences if his wishes were refused.

The little orphan boy went down from his high hill to the town to become son of the big chief there.

All this happened several years before we missionaries went into the district.

The boy was given a name by the chief. It was a slave name, Nasamu. Samu, to find; Na, I—I have found. Thus the literal meaning of this boy's name betrayed his position as slave: Nasamu—I have found one. For a long time the boy did not know the meaning of his own name.

Nasamu was set to work as horse boy. He would have to go and find fresh grass for the horse of the big chief. In the dry season this would be quite a task and might mean that Nasamu would have to walk a long way to some stream, in order to find fresh green grass. He would also have to clean the hut where the horse had its abode. It is not a mean hut that would be given to the animal. Such an animal would get better care than most of the children of the big chief. And should the horse die, it would provoke more anxiety and concern than should a wife die. A horse is more valuable than a woman. It is easier to get a new wife than to get a new horse. A woman may quarrel with her husband and make him weary with many words, but a horse will carry his master and spare him all weariness.

After a while Nasamu became aware of the fact that he was a slave rather than a son; that the chief was his taskmaster rather than his father. But there could be no thought of escape. Day after day he cut grass and swept the hut of the horse. He must be content to eat such things as were set before him, and much of his food consisted of native beer. A few cast-off tattering rags was all the covering he had for his body.

One day he heard a piece of strange news. He heard that in the town of Takum was a school, and that "a certain one" was teaching the people about God—the God Who made them—and that "the certain one" held a thing in his hand which was called "a book." This news made Nasamu's heart beat fast with desire to hear about the God Who made him. Would he dare to ask the chief for permission to come to that school? Yes, one evening he had the courage and went to the place where the chief was sitting.

"Lion, Lion," said Nasamu, clapping his hands to greet the chief. A chief is addressed in this way to honor him with power and authority.

"Nasamu, is that you?" responded the chief of the boy who was now a young man.

"Lion, yes, it is I, and, if you will agree to let me speak, I have a request."

"What is it you want?"

"Lion, I hear that in this your town one is telling of a Book and of a God Who made us. May I go to learn?"

"No, you may not go. Your work is to care for the horse. You may go and leave me."

Nasamu had to rise and leave the chief. He was heartbroken, his hopes crushed, but he returned to his hut where he slept together with several others. Day after day his heart still longed to go to school, and after a time he gathered up courage to go a second time to the chief and beg for permission.

Bowing to the ground, he respectfully greeted the chief with the same words, "Lion, Lion," meanwhile clapping his hands.

"Is it you, Nasamu? And what is your errand?"

"Lion, I have come again to ask you, if you will agree, to let me go to school and hear about God and the Book."

"Nasamu, look at *me*! See the wives I have; see the large compound I have; see the power I have. I do not know about the Book. And who are you? Why do you want to learn of something that I do not know about? Nasamu, I will give you a wife and you can settle down and rest your mind about school."

"Lion, it is not a wife I ask for, but I do want to go to school."

This second time his request was not granted. He was sent away. A little later the chief gave him a young girl—a Dzompere girl—to be his wife. Quite likely this girl also was a slave, and the chief did not desire her for himself, and so passed her on to Nasamu. All this happened before we missionaries came to the district. A convert from another town had been sent to Takum to work as a teacher-evangelist in that big town, preparatory to the coming of the missionaries.

But the Holy Spirit gives a person no rest when that one is to come to the knowledge of Christ. And so Nasamu was made to be bold and fearless. A third time, under the cover of night, he sought the presence of the chief, and greeted him as before.

"Lion, Lion," clapping his hands loudly to give honor and respect.

"It is Nasamu, and what have you come for at this time?"

"Lion, even if you cut my body in pieces, I must go to school and learn about the Book and about God."

The chief saw that this boy was not to be put off, and no doubt the Lord overruled to have the chief give Nasamu permission.

"Nasamu, I will let you go, but you must do your full share of work just the same. You are not to stay at the school by night. You are to come here and sleep.

"Lion, thank you, thank you!" said Nasamu as he arose to leave the chief.

He was very happy, and the next day he sought the Christian teacher who at once commenced to help him.

All the instruction was in Hausa, and Nasamu did not know anything about this language. He only knew the Dzompere, and a little Jukun. But he learned readily. First the alphabet, then a few exercises which were printed on sheets of paper, and then the first primer. Nasamu was learning many things at once, a new language, reading, writing—and the Truth of God.

How wonderful is the providence of God! When the missionaries came to the district, here was Nasamu, a Dzompere man, but with a knowledge of the Hausa language. In this way he was very useful as interpreter. The missionaries knew Hausa, but the Dzompere language was still untouched. Using an interpreter to preach the gospel is not desirable unless the interpreter is an earnest follower of the Lord Jesus. Even then it is not the ideal way, but must often be resorted to in the early stages of the work. And here then was a Christian interpreter. Here was the first convert from the Dzompere tribe!

Nasamu had not gone long to the mission school when he felt led to give up all the worship of his ancestors and declare himself to be "on the Lord's side."

When the missionaries came to the district a friendly relationship was established between the big chief and themselves. The chief was asked whether he would set Nasamu at liberty to work for the missionary, to help with the language, interpretation, etc., etc. This request was readily granted, and Nasamu, his wife and their first baby, moved their home from Takum to Lupwe, to be on the mission compound.

At this time Nasamu was an inquirer, having made his first public confession to follow Christ. We continued to give him instruction, and it seemed very evident that this first convert was thoroughly sincere. Before Rev. Whitman left the district on furlough, he had the joy of baptizing this first convert from the Dzompere tribe, dropping his slave name and giving him the name Danyelu (Daniel).

Danyelu's wife has also made confesssion of Christ. She is at present a catechumen, and we hope will receive baptism some time next year ('27). When I returned to the field after my first furlough I helped her with the birth of their second child.

When we came to decide upon three married baptized men, who were to be given the position of elder in the little flock, Danyelu was chosen to be one of the three. So far as we knew, these three men were honorable in every way, and had a clean record from the time they first made confession of Christ.

Later on, having no resident evangelist at Takum, we asked Danyelu to act as caretaker there. The mission has several huts and a chapel in Takum, and it is necessary to keep this place in good order. We also wanted Danyelu to buy the food at the native market for the boarding school, and to bring this out to Lupwe.

But on the hills around us were thousands of Dzompere people about whom we felt concerned. We made it a definite matter of prayer for a long time, and were led to ask that Danyelu might be separated unto special service among his own people. In Takum were several Christians who could witness to the Lord, but beyond our compound were thousands of Dzompere scattered over the hills without a single witness to lead them to the Christ. Trekking through the hills is very difficult, and many of the people can hear the message of life only once in a single year.

We realized that for Danyelu this would mean a great act o
self-denial. The Christians enjoy the fellowship of one another
and Danyelu would have to take his whole household and be the
only Christian in the midst of a heathen community. He would
have to earn his living by farming, and it might be hard for a
few years as the heathen would not help him unless he paid then
with beer, which, as a Christian, he would not be permitted to
do. Isolated on one of the hills, away from the native market, he
could not earn such a good living, and now he had himself, hi
wife and two little girls to feed and clothe. Knowing thes
things we yet realized that God was able to supply his need, and
that Jesus for our sakes became poor, and that Danyelu possessed
the supreme blessing of salvation.

One day he came to Lupwe bringing the food he had pur
chased in the native market, and I asked him to come in and
listen to a message I wished to tell him. He sat on the mat, and
I proceeded to tell him all that was upon my heart, and how
for a long time, my co-worker and I had been praying definitel;
for him. I said something like this: "Danyelu, there are no
less than ten thousand Dzompere people over these hills. It i
our task to tell them of Jesus Christ. Of all these ten thousand
the Lord God, in his infinite love and wisdom, has chosen you to
be the first to come to a knowledge of the Savior. Into you
darkness God came with the light of His Son Jesus. Now what
about the many thousands still in darkness? You, Danyelu, ar
responsible in part for this task of bringing them the light. Wil
you go home and pray about the matter, to see if God would hav
you move your home from Takum to one of these Dzomper
places?"

He looked rather surprised, and said he did not see that i
would be possible. I said: "You cannot see it until you hav
prayed about it. Therefore go home and make it a matter o
definite prayer."

About two or three weeks later he asked if I had time for
little talk. He then told me how that he had thought of the mat
ter over and over, and prayed about it, but he was afraid the
whole family would die of starvation.

I explained that it would be hard for a few years. He would receive no remuneration from the mission as we were building the work on the basis of a self-supporting native church; and if he went as a paid evangelist the heathen would not understand, and would say that he was coming to them with "white man's book and receiving much white man's money." This would be a decided hindrance to them in listening to the message. But, after a few years of seed-sowing, we would expect the gospel to bear fruit. If, through Danyelu's efforts converts were won, they would also be taught to tithe, and with these tithe offerings Danyelu could receive some help. I made this all very clear to him, and assured him that the work would be under close supervision of the missionary in charge of the district. I further urged him to go home and once more consider the matter.

The next day was Sunday, and I went in to Takum to take the Sunday meetings. Danyelu usually boils a kettle of water for tea which I have with a sandwich that I take along. He came and said that he "had words to make if I could let him speak." I gladly gave him the opportunity to say what he wanted. "You know, Baturiya, God called Moses to do a great work," he said, "but Moses refused to obey. He made excuses about his tongue and his mouth, but at last he did obey and was willing. Now, I have been just like Moses. I have refused and made excuses, but now I want to tell you that I am willing to go and try."

What a glorious victory! You may know how happy the missionaries were on this Sunday. We praised the Lord for sending His Spirit into Danyelu's heart to persuade him to go and witness for Christ to his own tribesmen.

After a little more conversation, Danyelu said, "Where do you think I should go, Baturiya?"

"To the west of us, nine miles, is Kwamba. You know how eagerly the people have listened whenever we visit them with the gospel. You remember," I continued, "how a man there pleaded with me to help his boy who was so sick. We told this man of our God Who has ears and can hear, eyes and can see, and that we would pray and ask Him to heal the boy. You remember he boy got well again and how glad the father was when we

came the next time to the village. And then near Kwamba ar
two other large hills, with many Dzompere people, which yo
could visit from Kwamba. I think you would do well to live i
Kwamba."

"Very well, we shall go to Kwamba," he said.

After speaking with the chief of the district about the matter
my co-worker and I went to Kwamba to see the chief and th
people there. Telling them that Danyelu was going to come an
live in their village, I asked them whether they were willing t
erect a hut—a prayer hut—where they might gather and hear th
word of the Lord. Before we left that day we saw the place marke
off where a small square building was to be put up by the peop
themselves, wherein they might gather to be instructed in th
things that lead to life eternal. Their willingness was also
great joy to us.

Then we called the two elders and asked them whether th
Christians of Takum should not have a share in helping the
brother to go out as the first voluntary worker in our distric
They were willing at once, and said, "Baturiya, let us, from ou
offerings take enough money to build the huts for Danyelu. On
hut for them to live and sleep in, and the other hut for his wi
to do the grinding and cooking." And so it was decided.

All the huts were completed, Danyelu with his wife, Haw
and with their two little girls, rose up from Takum and walke
over to Kwamba, nine miles. It was a couple of weeks after m
co-worker and I left the district that these Christians went t
Kwamba. Hawa had come to me weeping, "Who will help m
when you are gone?" She was soon to be confined, and so it wa
only natural that she would desire our help. But I assured he
that we would pray and ask the Lord to undertake for he
And this prayer was wonderfully answered. The first night the
slept in their new home at Kwamba, a little boy was born. I
writing me of it, Danyelu said: "We have come to Kwamba. Th
first night we were here the Lord gave us a son. I was alo
with Hawa. We are very thankful to the Lord for this gift of
son. I am so happy. We are calling our son *Job*."

You may wonder where he got the name Job. It made me smile. But I remember that we had been talking about Job just before I left. We do not have the Book of Job translated in the Hausa language, but I explained to them a little of the story of Job, emphasizing his wonderful faith and patience in the midst of great sorrow and suffering. This appealed to Danyelu, and when his first son was born, he decided to call him Job.

Danyelu has seen some of the cruelties of their heathen practices. He witnessed the killing of the women who were tied to the palm tree and speared to death. He knows a good deal about "the poison cup."

As yet nothing can be said about his work at Kwamba. One thing we know, and that is that as Christians we need to circle about him a girdle of strong intercession. His is no easy task!

Every month he is to be visited by the other two elders so they may keep in touch with his welfare and continue to encourage and help him.

May there be many more of the converts who will be willing to go out as Danyelu and become voluntary workers among their own people.

Danyelu has specially asked me to plead with the people in our home church to pray for him. Thus I pass on to you this personal request from the first convert of the Dzompere tribe who has now become the first voluntary worker among his own people.

While we acknowledge with praise that "the Lord has done great things for us whereof we are glad," let us continue to

"Pray without ceasing."

Not our ancestors. African monkeys.
See page 116.

CHAPTER XIX

"And a little child shall lead them."

CHAPTER XIX

"SUFFER THE LITTLE CHILDREN TO COME."

It was a heavy cold rain. I sat in my hut with a sweater on (we never have occasion to need a fire), and happened to look out of the window. Along the path I saw a few people hurrying to get home. Upon close observation I saw a man, no doubt a husband and father. He walked first, and carried nothing more than a long spear. The idea is that if he should see any animal, he could at once spear it. Then came a woman. On her head was a large basket. No doubt they had been in to the Takum market. On her back a little baby was fastened. The basket helped just a little to keep some of the cold rain off the baby. Of course none of the natives know such a thing as an umbrella. Then followed another little fellow. I was sorry for him. He was entirely naked, and he could hardly keep up with the two grown-ups who were able to walk along so fast. The little boy was trying to run, and then would slack a little. He looked so tired. He dared not be left far behind, for he would be afraid. He looked only about five or six years old. Rushing his little bare feet over the wet ground, with the rain pattering all over his body, he made a journey of not less than six miles. If that man knew the love of Jesus, do you think he would have carelessly left his little boy to plod along like this? Or would he have taken the little fellow in his arms and carried him?

Another time I came to a farm village. There were a few tiny huts where the people slept while doing their farm work. A woman was pounding corn. Out of a big tree a piece is cut, and then a hole scooped, wherein the corn is put. Then with a heavy stick the woman pounds the corn. Tied to the woman's back was a little baby. It looked only a couple of months old.

The fierce rays of the tropical sun were beating down on the baby's head. And every time the mother pounded with the big stick into the heavy wooden basin, the little babe's head would be thrown against her spine. Would our Christian mothers give their babies such thoughtless and unconcerned treatment?

"Salama, Salama" (Peace, Peace), I called out as I entered one of the compounds in the town of Takum. A mother was sitting prepared to give her wee boy a bath. She greeted me and smiled pleasantly, and offered me her little stool to sit on. Beside her was a clay basin that contained about a cupful of water. She put some water in the palm of her hand, and then held her hand close to the little fellow's mouth. Her hand acted as a dipper to give the baby a drink. Then she laid him flat on her lap, and from the basin she took a mouthful of water herself. Then she spit this water on the body of her boy and began to rub with her hand. One mouthful gone, she took a second mouthful and continued this until the water was finished and until the whole body of the baby was wet. No soap, no wash-cloth, no towel.

Returning to the mission compound I saw Astira giving her baby a bath. She had an enamel basin, and she had warmed the water. She set the baby right in the basin and gave it such a lovely wash. The baby splashed and enjoyed it. What made the difference? The first woman was a heathen. The second mother has been a Christian for some years, and the gospel is helping to influence every part of her life.

I explained to you that the heathen exchange their children. A man has a child, and he brings it to the home of his brother to be brought up. The brother has a child and gives it to this man to bring up. Sometimes the child is given to its grandparents to be trained. In this way the child receives harsher treatment. How often I have heard a little one screaming with fear as most unsuitable discipline would be administered. But our Christians promise before God not to give their children to another for training, but to take this responsibility themselves. And I see the little ones of our Christians folding their hands and closing their eyes as they thank the Lord for the dish of food before them. I hear their little voices singing: "Jesus loves me, this I know." And on Sunday I see the mother often sit down with her family and have a little Sunday School with them. Then my heart aches for the thousands of heathen children, and I cannot help but ask when they will hear of Jesus who said, "Suffer the little children to come unto Me."

The mortality among children is very high in Central Africa. It is quite certain that fully half the children who are born die before they reach the age of five. There are no doctors and hospitals. There is no drug store to get medicine when a little one gets a high fever or a very heavy cold. Many of the mothers have not sufficient nourishment for their children, and such weak children have no chance to fight malaria, dysentery, etc. The parents also are very ignorant. They continue to feed the child coarse and heavy food even when it is ill. The sick body should rest, it cannot take care of digesting such food, and soon the baby dies.

What a comfort our Christians have when they know the Lord and know how to pray. I just received a letter from one of the elders of our little flock in which he said: "Our boy was very sick. We thought he was going to die. For five days and five nights we (his wife and himself) cried unto Jehovah. And Jehovah saw the sorrow of our hearts and healed our boy. He is well again, and we are so very thankful to our God."

At a certain compound I heard loud wailing one day, and enquired what was the reason. I was told that a little boy had just died and all the people of the compound had gathered to wail with the father and mother. What an empty, hopeless wail! Not a single ray of comfort! A little hole dug in the compound, the wee corpse rolled in a grass mat, put in the hole, covered over, and the funeral is finished!

Contrast with that the death of a child from the family of one of our baptized Christians. True, there was weeping, but there was a submission to God's will. There was real sorrow, but this sorrow was mingled with hope. They believed that Jesus—the Lover of little children—had taken their child to Himself. The other Christians gathered to help their bereaved brother. They dug the grave, and cared for the corpse. They had a little funeral, singing, Scripture and prayer. While no missionaries were there at the time, they knew what was the proper thing for them, as Christians, to do. They believe that Jesus gathered this little lamb and carried it safely to His heavenly home.

> "But thousands and thousands who wander and fall
>   Never heard of that Heavenly home;
> I should like them to know there is room for them all,
>   And that Jesus has bid them to come.
> I long for that blessed and glorious time,
>   The fairest and brightest and best,
> When the dear little children of every clime
>   Shall crowd to His arms and be blest."

You will not be surprised that sometimes the missionary feels crushed by all the suffering of heathendom. One cannot be in such a dark spot and be unmindful of the fact that every day people are dying—children and older folks—who have not been acquainted with the Savior.

On the other hand we are encouraged to know that our King is marching on to victory. We have great expectation from the children that are being born to the converts in our district. We look for that day when they will establish Christian homes, and, by faith, we see the gospel, through their efforts, go forward by leaps and bounds.

It is a joy to come into the chapel on a Sunday morning and see the children gather—most of them able to walk, but some of them tied to the mother's back. It is a delight to see the older ones help along with the singing, and drop a small coin, called an "anini" (one-fifth of a penny) into the collection plate. It sometimes makes me smile as I look over their faces and think of their names. They have Bible names. So often a parent will come to me and say, "Will you please name our new baby?" I always give them three or four names to choose from. But sometimes they have the name all ready, because they have been impressed with the story of the character.

Last year we were dedicating a little boy. Rev. Guinter was with us for special services. I asked the father what he had decided to call the boy. He said, "Baturiya, I wish him to be called 'Simon'." To make sure I repeated it, "Simon is the name you want?" Then he promptly replied, "Of course I mean 'Simon Peter'." This was the first time anyone took two names, but I think this Christian was under the impression that Simon Peter was a single name, not to be separated.

I would like the pleasure of introducing you to a dozen of the little children, born of Christian parents, in our district:

Hausa Name	English	Parents
Febe	Phebe	Filibbus and Astira
Ibrahim	Abraham	Filibbus and Astira
Samuila	Samuel	Filibbus and Astira
Ishaku	Isaac	Istifanus and Mariyamu
Rifkatu	Rebekah	Istifanus and Mariyamu
Siman Bitrus	Simon Peter	Istifanus and Mariyamu
Hannatu	Hannah	Danyelu and Hawa
Tabitha	Tabitha	Danyelu and Hawa
Ayuba	Job	Danyelu and Hawa
Ishaya	Isaiah	Gombe and Saya
Karneliya	Cornelia	Gombe and Saya
Luka	Luke	Gombe and Saya

There are quite a few more, but this will give you an example of the variety of names.

Not any of the children from the district who have been to our boarding school are mentioned.

You will agree that we have reason to be hopeful for the future. We look at all these little lives, children of our converts plus the boys in the boarding school, and pray that God may draw them to love the Lord Jesus while they are young, and not to depart from His way as they grow older.

May the day soon dawn when the heathen children all over the world will hear the glad song:

> "There's a Friend for little children,
> Above the bright blue sky,
> A Friend that never changes,
> Whose love will never die."

Helping the missionary on "blue Monday."
See page 144.

CHAPTER XX

*"Fear thou not; for I am with thee:
be not dismayed; for I am thy God:
I will strengthen thee; yea, I will
help thee; yea, I will uphold thee
with the right hand of my right-
eousness."*

ISAIAH 41:10

CHAPTER XX

A FEW QUESTIONS ANSWERED

It is quite natural that many questions would arise in your mind when you hear the different missionaries on furlough speak of their work in heathen lands. Therefore I have decided to devote this one chapter to answer some of the questions asked me from time to time by the friends here in the homeland. I feel sure that many questions have already been answered in the preceding chapters. But here are a few more:

How do you get your mail?

There is no postoffice in our district, but there is a sub-station (with a native clerk in charge) at our head station, Ibi, seventy-five miles from our mission compound. This makes it necessary for me to send to Ibi for my mail. We send a man every two weeks. We put all our letters in a wooden box that has a good cover and a padlock. We lock it and retain the key. The carrier takes the box on his head and starts off to walk to Ibi—seventy-five miles. The missionary there has a duplicate key to our box, opens it, takes out the mail and sends it to the postoffice, and then he puts back into the box such mail as is waiting there for us. The box is again locked, and the same man carries it back. It takes a carrier a week (six days) to make this journey of one hundred and fifty miles. For this service he receives the sum of one dollar. If the box is heavy we may give him ten cents extra.

* * *

Where do you buy your food?

Before going to the field I take a trip to Chicago and order from Montgomery, Ward & Co. (they do special packing for export purposes) several cases of tinned goods: milk, flour (the flour is packed in ten-pound tins), coffee, tea, sugar, dried fruits, jams, cereals, some tinned vegetables and fruits, and a few other necessities. The price of such an order is exactly doubled by the time it reaches Lupwe station. Special packing, ocean freight, inland river freight, and then each box carried seventy-five miles into the bush, makes imported food very high. We use as much native food as possible: fowls, goats, sheep, and sometimes beef can be had from the native market. Due to the heat, improper feeding, etc., the meat does not have the same taste as at home. The meat is generally tough and dry, and never has any fat. Sweet potatoes, yams, brown rice, pumpkins, peanuts, onions, beans, and eggs can all be bought very cheaply in the market. The eggs are smaller than ours at home, because all the fowls are very small. The eggs cost one cent each. A fowl can be bought for a quarter. On the compound we have several banana trees, mango trees, and pawpaw. We also have pineapples. These fruit are brought in from home (except the banana, which the natives grow, though a different variety from ours).

* * *

Why do you live in round mud huts?

It being a warm climate we never need be concerned about cold and drafts. We cannot have a wooden structure because the white ants would soon destroy it. We might have a stone and cement building. This would be very expensive, as all the cement would have to be imported from home. It would require a missionary who understands building work to put up such a place. But you must remember that Lupwe is a new station. We are not certain that this is the permanent site for the mission station. It may be that after ten or fifteen years we shall want to have the station some other place in the district. For this reason we put up what might be called temporary buildings. We shall then not be bound by expensive property should we care to abandon this place and go elsewhere in the district.

* * *

Is there no missionary in the district now?

For the past three years we have been two women workers, Miss Haigh from England was with me for nearly two years, when her health demanded that she go on furlough. Belonging to the British branch she was sent to one of their stations up on the plateau, where the altitude is several hundred feet higher than Lupwe, and the climate is drier and colder. Then Miss Walker, of the Canadian branch was sent to be with me for a year. We came home together as far as England. She was married and is now returning to the field, her husband to take charge of a new station under the Canadian branch of our mission, working in French Africa. Rev. Wm. Hood, of the Southern Presbyterian Church, U. S. A., was given charge at Lupwe for this year. As soon as I return he is to go home on furlough. This is his first term of service on the field. At the present time I have no idea as to who is to be with me at Lupwe next term.

*   *   *

What is the "poison cup" or the "poison ordeal"?

Many, many people have been killed by the poison ordeal, or by drinking the poison cup. It belongs to the darkness of the fetish worship. We have a kind of cactus in our district which is deadly poisonous. It is extracted and used to put on arrows when the men go shooting. The poison will infect the blood and the animal is sure to die.

But this poison has also been used to kill people. It would be administered to them in food or drink after the witch-doctor pronounced the death sentence upon anyone who was said to be possessed with an evil spirit.

The converts tell me that in our district the hair from the mustache of a leopard would be used to kill people. One such hair, cut into very small pieces, would be mixed into a dish of food. This would be given to the person who was to be killed, and without knowing it, he would be eating all this ground hair. This hair is very sharp, and no doubt it perforates the intestines. We are told that a person to whom this evil-spirit cure was given would soon become very sick. Then the whole abdomen would become distended with swelling, and the person would die.

Thousands of lives, men, women and little children, have been cut off by the use of the poison ordeal.

Are you ever afraid of the people, or of the cannibals?

Thus far I have had very little reason to be afraid of the people. It is necessary that the missionary continually hold an attitude of superiority. Not in the sense of "we are better than you." God forbid! But rather in the sense of claiming and using authority. The missionary must prove himself or herself to be "boss" (not bossy); commanding and demanding obedience. We must seek the Lord to endow us with the gifts of leadership.

It does not take long before the people know that we are there for their personal welfare. We do not come to collect tax, or to buy their products for trading purpose; we come to help them. And it does not take long for them to feel whether or not we truly *love* them. *Love* will always be a drawing power; *love* will bring almost any battle to a victorious finish.

To work in this part of Africa it is necessary that I obtain a permit from the British government. This permit also assures me of their protection. Since the government has taken over these protectorates, tribal wars belong to the history of the past. We hope that soon cannibalism and all forms of infanticide and witch-doctor cruelties will be abolished.

* * *

Are you afraid of the animals and snakes?

Many a time have I trembled at these. It makes a difference as to the state of one's physical and nervous energy. One may be running a low malaria temperature for days, or be recovering from an attack of fever, or be very tired and needing rest or furlough. At such a time thunder storms and other disturbances are apt to affect one.

However afraid I may be of the howl of the leopard, I am still more afraid of the howls of human beings. It is easier to kill a snake than to still the "temper" of some human beings. To hear a man and his wife fighting with each other in the compound or in some village; so raging mad as to lose all self-control; acting as if they were truly demon-possessed—this makes me more afraid. Then it is that I feel my own weakness against the powers of the evil one, who makes people act like roaring lions earing each other to pieces. At such a time one cries out, "O Lord, undertake! Give me of Thy strength!"

* * *

When they are converted, do they have any consciousness of sin?

Returning from prayer meeting at Takum on a Thursday morning, I found my co-worker looking rather pale. She had not been long in the district, and received a fright that morning. I asked what the trouble was, and she told me that two of the older boys (both inquirers, each one over twenty) had a fierce battle with each other that morning. Not having the language as yet, she was afraid to interfere. They were in school when I arrived. At once we made the matter one of definite prayer. I thought it wise not to call these youths at once, but to patiently pray about the matter a day or two. One of them came to my hut to ask a certain question. I called him inside, and said I wanted to talk to him a minute. "The other day," I said to him, "when I was in Takum, you and A—— had a fight together. I was very sorry to hear of this, and want you to tell me whether you are still angry with A——." He felt ashamed, but was glad to answer quickly: "Baturiya, we did fight; and we were angry with each other for most of the day. But at night we said, 'Let us forgive each other and ask God to forgive us also,' and we did that. We prayed together and confessed our anger to the Lord, and asked Him to forgive us and help us." So, as we prayed the Lord worked!

One Sunday I returned from Takum, having been there for the day, and one of my personal boys came to greet me. He said, "Are you tired, my mother?" I said, "Just a little." Then he asked, "Is your body tired or is your heart tired also?" (They understand that on some days we have wearying hours of discipline to wade through.) "I guess only my body is tired today," I said. He sat quiet for a little, and then said, "My mother, I have done something wrong, I must tell you, but I am afraid to tell you." I told him to go on and tell me. "Yesterday morning when I cut down a bunch of bananas that were getting ripe, four

bananas fell on the ground. I did not bring them into your house
I ate two and I gave two away. I know that that was stealing
Today when I sat in my hut reading my Bible, I thought of my
sin, and began to cry, and asked the Lord to help me tell you, and
ask you to forgive me. Will you agree to forgive me?" I asked
him to tell me honestly whether this was the first time he had
yielded to this temptation to steal anything since working for
me. He assured me it was. I talked to him for a little, and then
told him that we should ask the Lord to forgive him. We knelt
together, and I asked him to pray first. Not less than six times
over during his prayer did he tell the Lord that he had broken
the commandment and committed the sin of stealing. He began
to cry as he pleaded with the Lord not only to forgive him, but
to make his heart stronger to withstand all temptation. After
I prayed, I assured him that I had forgiven him, and that, upon
the ground of the promises in God's word, he might believe that
God had also forgiven him. He went away feeling grateful and
much relieved.

I could mention several matters like this to prove that more
and more, as they seek to follow the Lord in truth, the Holy
Spirit unveils to them their own sin, and quickens within them
repentance, the power to confess and seek forgiveness, in order
that they may know the "peace of God that passeth all under
standing."

*   *   *

Do the people appreciate the missionary and his efforts?

Yes, decidedly so! Most of those who come to the dispensary
are very grateful for all that we do for them.

A most hearty welcome is given us in the different villages
where our boarding school pupils live. The father and mother
of one pupil walked miles to come to our place and bring me
little present. The parents have told me to beat their children
if they did not obey me. And now in many of the villages, after
a few visits, we are able to gather the people in two different
groups. We have the women in a separate meeting from the
men. This proves that we are gaining their confidence. Other

wise the men would be afraid to have the women told anything outside their hearing.

The school pupils are very happy. And they do show appreciation. They know that we white folks are very fond of flowers. Bula, the baby in our school (whose picture is on page 228), was given me by his father. The father said: "I have had five children. All have died. Only this boy is left to me. I am giving you the last and all that I have. Please, white lady, take good care of him. If he dies, my hands will be empty." Bula is rather mischievous, but very bright. During the dry season there are very few flowers to be found. Bula went out, after we had the first one of two rains, to look for flowers. He found one pretty flower. A long stem, with several little bells of lavender and pale yellow, very much resembling a hyacinth. He proudly carried the flower to the compound, and came to me holding it out with a loud greeting to express that he was bringing me a present. It was only one flower; but it was a pretty touch of nature—the first flower I had in the room for a few months. And it was very thoughtful of this little boy, who has no pennies to buy a present, to show his love in this way.

During one year I went for a vacation to visit two mission stations which I had never before seen. I took one personal boy along to help me while traveling. At the first station, I was taken sick with flu and fever. In the evening my boy came into the hut to greet me and see if he could do anything for me. Then he began to cry. I asked him why he was crying; whether he was homesick, or hungry, or what was the matter. No, he was not homesick, nor was he hungry. Then it dawned upon me that he had never before seen me ill, and that it was sympathy. I said: "Are you crying because I am not well?" "Yes," he sobbed. I told him that it was kind of him to care about my health, but he did not need to weep. We would pray and ask the Lord to make me better. He left, and as I thought, went to retire. Several grains of quinine and aspirin kept me restless and awake. I was alone in a small hut that had a door of heavy grass matting. I kept the lantern burning all night, and no doubt this shone through the door. At one o'clock in the morning I heard a voice at the door, "Greetings, my mother, how do you feel in your body?" I told the boy he might come in and give me a drink of water. It would encourage him if he could do something for me. Then I said, "Have you been sitting outside there all this while?" "Yes, but that is nothing, I did not mind, I am not afraid," he answered. "Listen," I said to him, "now you go right to your hut and to sleep. I shall be all right, and shall try to sleep too. It is not necessary for you to sit outside there at this midnight hour." He left, and I tried to sleep. Did he go to his hut? Before dawn he was seen by one of the other missionaries on the compound still sitting in front of the hut, wrapped in his sleeping blanket. He had remained there the whole night. He thought I might want to call him, and was sure to be where he would hear that call. Surely that is more than *faithful service.* That is *love* and *appreciation!*

*   *   *

On Christmas Eve all the people on our compound were very excited. They had gone to the bush, hauled heavy pieces of dead trees to the compound to have a big log fire. They were singing the Christmas songs; playing some ring games; and were very happy. My co-worker and I decorated our huts with some green and red and silver paper that had been sent to us from the home friends. We were going to be as much in the spirit of the day out here in this bush station in Africa as we would be in America. It was a little later than usual when we retired, and we decided to sleep together that night. At midnight, we heard the voices of all our compound people singing softly at our door. They had quietly come up on the veranda, led by the teacher, Filibbus, and together began to sing the beautiful hymns of the Babe of Bethlehem! We have about six or eight Christmas hymns translated into Hausa. For weeks they had been practicing these hymns in school. An angel choir broke the stillness of night on that first Christmas; and here in Africa, with all the silence of the bush about us, suddenly we were awakened by the voices of those we love on *this* Christmas—so many many years after the Babe was born in Bethlehem. Did it make us glad? More than words can tell! No gold or silver could bring the joy that we had that night. We spoke little to each other, but we felt the force of the words, "My cup runneth over."

That same night, after singing at our door, several of the older boys, accompanied by the teacher, walked in to Takum. They went to surprise the Christians there. It was surely a surprise to them at Takum, and they appreciated it that the Lupwe people walked four miles at midnight to come and give them this pleasure. Then the entire group, Takum Christians together with the delegation from Lupwe, went to the place of the chief and sang at the entrance of his compound. This was about two o'clock in the morning. Then they went to a few other compounds and sang Christmas carols at their entrance huts. After that the Takum people went to sleep, while the Lupwe folks walked four miles to get back home.

As soon as we missionaries were up in the morning, little voices were on hand to greet us with "Blessing to this Christmas Day!" Little presents were brought to us, sent by the older ones, and accompanied by little messages of love and greetings.

After breakfast we all went in to Takum, to have a service there. The chapel was crowded that morning. Everybody was shining without because of large quantities of oil rubbed all over their body, but they were shining within with the spirit of the day as well. Such hearty singing! Such radiant faces! Such joyous greetings! And a special love-offering to show our gratitude to Him Whose birthday we were celebrating!

The Takum Christians arranged to have all the Lupwe pupils and others stay with them for the day. They arranged for a noon meal, and after that for games and play.

We missionaries returned home, to have a quiet afternoon. We were inexpressibly happy! Had not the Lord Jesus promised that those who leave all for His sake and the gospel would receive in this life a *hundred-fold reward*. This fullness of joy—the joy of the Lord—the joy of seeing men and women truly transformed by the power of the gospel—this is the *"hundred-fold reward."*

Python and leopard in life and death struggle. See page 111.

CHAPTER XXI

"The night lies dark upon the earth, and we have light;
So many have to grope their way, and we have sight;
One path is theirs and ours—of sin and care,
But we are borne along, and they their burden bear;
Footsore, heart-weary, faint they on the way,
Mute in their sorrow, while we kneel and pray;
Glad are they of a stone on which to rest,
While we lie pillowed on the Father's breast.

"Father, why is it that these millions roam,
And guess that that is Home, and urge their way?
Is it enough to keep the door ajar,
In hope that some may see the gleam afar,
And guess that that is Home, and urge their way
To reach it haply, somehow and some day?
May not I go, and lend them of my light?
May not mine eyes be unto them for sight?
May not the brother-love Thy love portray?
And news of Home make Home less far away?"

REV. R. WRIGHT HAY

CHAPTER XXI

PROBLEMS AND DIFFICULTIES

"The problems confronting us just now, friends, are like a mere ripple compared to the great waves of difficulty which are to roll down upon us as our work progresses." So spoke one of the missionaries—who has been much used of God in the Sudan—at a Field Council meeting that I attended. For a long time I pondered upon this statement, made by a man of several years experience, and the more I think of it, the more I see the truth and significance of that word.

Should all the missionaries in Africa be asked: "What is the greatest problem confronting the messenger of the cross in this dark land?" I believe that, with very few exceptions, the answer would be: "Polygamy."

Polygamy is practised by the Mohammedans as well as by the heathen all over Africa. To my knowledge there is only one mission society in all Africa that will permit the sacrament of baptism being administered to a polygamist.

Very often a man is kept waiting for ten years before he receives baptism, and that for no other reason except that he has more than one wife. It may be that he had these plural wives before he was converted, but even so, he is not allowed to enter the fellowship of the church until he comes to live with only one wife.

Some people at home have thought that to be wrong policy on the part of the missionaries. If it were wrong policy, we could hardly think of so many missionary societies being guided to take such wrong action, and to enforce such wrong regulations for church membership. The fact that every society—with the exception of one small organization—is united in its opinion upon this matter, would help us to believe that this guidance was of the Holy Spirit.

Supposing we tolerated polygamy. See what would result. A young unmarried man wants to make confession. He knows that if he does so at once, he will be allowed to have only one wife. He would naturally conclude that it would be to his advantage to wait three or four years. By that time he might have two wives, and then he would come and declare his allegiance to Christ. He would not be asked to give up one of his wives. Polygamy is profitable; and who will not seek personal gain? A man will likely have more children if he has more than one wife. The women will help him with the farm work; and so he can have a larger farm. Later on the children will also help him to farm, and to trade. A man having many wives and many children is looked upon as a "big man." So he also gains honor for himself. If a Christian were allowed to retain his many wives, wherein would our religion differ from Mohammedanism and the heathen religions?

Now we do not tolerate polygamy. See then what difficulty is before the missionary.

A man having four wives is converted. He asks permission to declare publicly his faith in Christ. This is granted; and he becomes an inquirer. But he is told that he must put away three of his wives, and keep only one. I believe it is not always insisted upon that he keep the first wife. An easy way would be for that man to sell three of his wives as quickly as possible. May he sell them to become the second or third wife of some heathen man? Certainly not. Putting them out of polygamy with himself into the same state with another man would not be honoring to our Christian teaching. Sometimes a woman is very angry when her husband becomes a Christian, and she runs away to her parents. She asks her parents to find another husband for her. In such a case a Christian is not responsible for her action. On the other hand, supposing two of the four wives are converted and also publicly confess to follow the Lord Jesus. What is to be done then? He may choose one such Christian to remain with him, to be his only legal wife. But a place must be found for the other Christian woman. These plural wives cannot be dismissed to live by themselves. With the state of morality as it is in Africa no woman can live pure for any length of time unless she knows that she is under authority. For a Christian to dismiss his plural wives without having made provision for them is like casting them upon the street to become prostitutes. In the case of a Christian wife, he is bound by Christian duty to find a Christian husband for her. If she is young, this is not an impossibility. Young men are coming into the Christian church who are glad to find a Christian helpmate; and they are often not unwilling to take a woman who has been previously married. But the missionary will be expected to help in all these tangled matrimonial affairs.

A further difficulty arises with the children. If a man has four wives, and each wife has borne him children, who are to claim possession of these children? Supposing a wife runs off to her parents, and takes her child with her. Will the Christian husband be permitted to claim that child? It is his child also; and becoming a Christian, dare he see his child brought up as a heathen? If one of his wives is converted, and he finds a Christian husband for her, will he let her take her children along? This is a very complicated problem.

The solving of these problems depends largely upon the missionary. He is the spiritual guide to the converts. The missionary, conscious of his weakness, depends upon the Holy Spirit to guide him aright.

* * *

Closely related to this problem of polygamy is the difficulty of the marriage customs and marriage ceremonies. A goodly number of young men, of marriageable age, are continually found among the group of believers. Being Christians, are we allowed to sanction their marrying heathen girls? In our district we are facing this problem at the present time. We know it is desirable that these young men shall marry Christian girls. But there are no Christian girls. The work is still in the earliest pioneer stage. Must we say to these young men: "Seeing there are no Christian girls, you must not marry." We have no right to bind them in this fashion. Then there is only one thing left to do—and that is to permit them to take unto themselves heathen girls. They will have a very hard time to get the consent of heathen parents to marry their daughter to a Christian. In many tribes it is customary for sacrifices to be offered to the spirits previously to the girl's marriage, asking the spirits to not withhold from her the blessing of motherhood. Heathen parents will ask the girl to take part in these sacrifices, and will always ask the young man who wishes to marry her whether he worships the spirits.

Being a Christian, he will testify that he worships the true and living God, and that he will expect his wife to also abandon spirit worship. You can understand how few heathen would consent to their daughter marrying a Christian on this basis.

We have had quite a few of our young men converts marry heathen girls. But I am thankful to say that in nearly every case the girl has come to believe in Jesus Christ, and has forsaken the worship of her parents.

Here is a young man who gets the consent of the parents to marry their daughter. He begins to get the dowry ready. This dowry varies in different tribes. I already said that among the Dzompere the dowry is thirty sheep or thirty goats for a young unmarried girl. When the dowry is paid, there is an agreement made which cannot be broken that this girl is to be his wife. This agreement to us is like an engagement. But the young man has the right to call the girl his wife. The people outside also refer to her as "the wife of So and So." But she is still with her parents. They keep her until such time as they decide it is fitting for her to go to the compound of her husband and take up the duties of a wife. When they send her away from her parental home a big feast will be made. This is the wedding. A public ceremony is performed.

Now the young man claims that the girl is his legal wife as soon as he pays the dowry in full. The missionaries rather assert that she is not his wife until such time as the parents consent for her to go and live with him. Here is a serious difference of opinion. If, a few months after the public wedding, this girl becomes mother, is the Christian husband subject to the discipline of the church or not?

What kind of a ceremony do they have? Before a company of people the bride crawls to the groom and hands him a dish of food. By this act she declares herself willing to become his wife. He puts forth two hands to receive the dish of food from her, and by so doing he testifies that he accepts her as his wife and declares to be her husband. Each tribe will have its own customs and ceremonies. This is common in our district.

Now this is altogether too loose. We must have something more binding and more honorable for our Christians. So we have the rule that every convert will be expected to have a Christian marriage ceremony. He must come with his wife in the chapel, and they must answer the same questions as are contained in the ceremony used at home. He must also declare before God, the minister and the congregation that he proposes with all his heart to live with *one* wife. Because of the peculiar tendency of the land toward polygamy we feel it a duty to add this obligation. The minister then pronounces upon them the blessing of the church.

This sounds nice, but you will be surprised to hear that several of our Christians do not desire such a ceremony. They are not prepared to easily shake off all the customs of their fore-fathers, and throw them aside as dust. The government recognizes a native ceremony as being legal; and the man will often ask the missionary, "Do I need to be married twice over?" Also, the girl may be very ignorant, and we shall have to wait until she can be instructed as to the meaning of such a Christian ceremony, and what obligations it imposes upon her. She may stubbornly refuse to have such a binding ceremony. In the event that they refuse, what then? Then the inquirer or catechumen is taken off the roll until such time as he is willing to submit to the rules of the church. If he is a baptized member, he will be put under discipline and denied the privileges of the church: communion, dedication of his children; and he will not be permitted to have charge of any preaching services in the church or to be Sunday School teacher.

Last November we had the first Christian marriage ceremony in our district. Two couples stood in the chapel before the minister and the congregation to take their vows and receive the blessing of the church. We thank God for this victory; and we take courage!

*   *   *   *   *   *   *   *

In establishing a Christian church in a heathen land, we are continually confronted with the barriers of tribal custom.

We do not wish to make a long list of laws forbidding this, that and the other thing. We want to emphasize a positive message—"Believe in the Lord Jesus Christ and thou shalt be saved." But we find it necessary to enlighten our Christians on all matters wherein we have specific guidance in the Word of God. Due to the fact that they have not the whole Bible translated in their own language, we must give them verbal rules which are found in Scripture.

Take for example the custom of tribal marks. Nearly every tribe has certain peculiar marks to prove what tribe they belong to. A ten-day-old baby was brought to me one morning, and I counted no less than twelve marks on its body. These had been cut right into the flesh, and charcoal rubbed in to keep them distinct. I asked the mother when this was done, and she said that on the eighth day a man came and did it for them. It would be done over again when the child would become six months old, and then for a last time when the child would be about eight years old. It would then last for life, and everyone would know to what tribe that child belonged. There are marks for women as well as for men.

What stand must the Christian church take here? We have an express command of the Lord to the children of Israel that they were not to mark their bodies. So we tell our Christians that they are not to mark the bodies of their children. In no way are they to brand themselves or their offspring. A Christian father comes to me and says: "Then when my son grows up, no one will know to what tribe he belongs." Each man loves his own tribe; and it seems to me there is a little patriotism here. To them the tribal marks are something like the Stars and Stripes to us. I must try to explain that in Christ Jesus, the Dzompere believer and the Jukun believer are one. And that God has expresssly commanded His children not to abuse the body—which He has created—with any form of unnecessary torture. They must be taught that it is impossible for them to improve upon the work of the Almighty by decorations and tribal marks.

* * *

What about making tithing a *rule* in the African church? We do not have such a rule in our home church. When we make a rule we must demand enforcement. It becomes a serious matter when a church rule is broken. We are dealing with a "child race," and they need to be dealt with as children. The missionaries are not agreed upon this matter of what rules we shall enforce upon the converts. At present we teach tithing; but we do not demand it. That is, we do not discipline a man if he is slack in this respect. Human nature is quite the same the world over. Even among these primitive peoples in Africa we find some with a generous spirit; and some who are otherwise.

Already I told you about the rule of prohibition we have in our little flock. Not imposed upon the converts by the missionary, but decided by the baptized members.

As yet we have no organized church in our district. We are in the pioneer stage. As soon as we organize a church, it will be necessary to frame a constitution. Such a constitution will contain "Rules and Regulations." Already we are thinking of that day, though it seems a long way off. What a responsibility! To think of making a constitution that will be absolutely in harmony with the teachings of Holy Writ, and that will be a part of the foundation of the Church of Jesus Christ in that part of Africa! Surely the missionary needs wisdom from above.

* * *

Another great problem before us is the training of leaders from among the converts. We look forward to the future when we shall have a native ministry. *Today* is the time to begin to plan for their training. It is impossible to take a few converts and send them home to enter our colleges and seminaries to receive training. We must arrange to have them educated on the field.

Here is a man in our district—who has done at least five years faithful service as teacher-evangelist. He feels called to give his life to definite evangelistic work. How long must he serve before we can trust him to perform some of the special duties in the church? He now serves as elder, and also as evangelist. When will he be promoted? That is, when will we permit him to have charge of such a service as "dedicating the children of believers?" This is a public ceremony in the chapel, and thus far conducted only by an ordained missionary. How many years must this evangelist serve before he can become pastor or ordained minister, and be permitted to administer the sacraments.

Most of the missionaries agree that an evangelist must serve in that capacity, with a clean record, at least twenty years, before he can be ordained to the ministry. This I believe is the rule of the Reformed Church of South Africa in their work in Nyassaland. During this time the evangelist must receive training.

For such training we must have a special staff of workers. It is utterly impossible for a missionary who has the responsibility of the running of a station to give many hours each day to train such leaders. This work of training leaders is so important for the future progress of the work that we cannot afford to neglect it at the present time. However short of staff, we must make provision for the training of evangelists, who will eventually become the ministers among the people.

An ideal way is to have theoretical and practical training combined. A pupil would get one year of intensive school work, followed by two years of practical work under the supervision of a missionary. Then he would get a second year of school work, followed by three years of practical. The third year of school work should be followed by five years of practical.

An evangelist is always expected to have charge of a school if he is placed at an out-station, and thus his training should also include an extensive course in "pupil-teacher" work, under the supervision of an educational worker.

Surely your picture of a missionary standing comfortably under a palm tree—Bible in hand—surrounded by a group of heathen has changed.

There is no more glorious work in all the world than being called to be a messenger for the King. Is there a work that involves greater responsibility? Christian work has been called "the Service Royal." So it is. To be enlisted in the Service Royal one must be continually arrayed in the "whole armor of God";

> "Praying always with all prayer and supplication in the Spirit. . . ."

> "For we wrestle not against flesh and blood, but against principalities, against powers, against the rulers of the darkness of this world, against spiritual wickedness in high places. . . ."

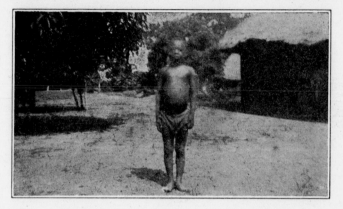

The baby of the boarding school. See page 213.

CHAPTER XXII

"He shall see of the travail of His soul, and shall be satisfied."

CHAPTER XXII

"IS IT NOTHING TO YOU?"

We are living in the year 1926 A.D., faced with the fact that more than one-half the population of the world is still untouched by any missionary effort whatsoever. Over half the people in the world have never had an opportunity to hear of Jesus Christ. *Is it nothing to you?*

*　　*　　*

Each year thousands upon thousands of people must pass through the dark valley of death without ever having heard the name of Jesus—that "Name all other names excelling." All their life they spent sitting in darkness, and alas, they die without ever having seen the faintest glimmer of the Light of Christ. *Is it nothing to you?*

*　　*　　*

"The world's great heart is aching" because of oppression; idolatry; false and superstitious religions; cruel bloodshed; disease without remedy; plague without help; sorrow without hope; physical torture without sympathy; painful suffering without balm; death without Jesus. *Is it nothing to you?*

*　　*　　*

For centuries the great heart of Africa has been groaning in silence. Only very recently are we entering in with the Sword of the Spirit, proclaiming to these millions, that God can heal their wounds, and forgive their sin. And many who sit in darkness and in the valley of death are seeing Jesus—the Light of the world.

We are indeed grateful that the chains of slavery are ceasing to be used, but let us remember that giving the captive physical liberty does not set his soul free. There is still the bondage of spiritual slavery. Only Jesus Christ can snap the coils that bind a person to that great master Slave-Dealer, the Devil.

I have told you of some who are turning to the light, who are entering into the glorious liberty of Christ, but, compared to the great masses of people, they are very few. Is it the "sound of marching in the tops of the mulberry trees" assuring us that victory is near?

"Ride on, O King Eternal . . . ."

We have been forced to close some of our stations because of lack of funds and lack of missionaries. At other stations the staff has been cut down. This is the cry everywhere today. The largest denominations in America—faced with a growing deficit in their missionary effort—will have to call home a great number of workers from the different fields next year. With all the luxury that we have in our beloved homeland today, must the cause of Christ thus suffer loss?

And away out there in Africa are still many tribes absolutely untouched—thousands of villages unreached—millions of people unacquainted with the message of salvation. *Is it nothing to you?*

* * *

As you see your children in all the excitement and joy of Christmas open their parcels; and as you hear them sing the beautiful carols—remember that there are millions of children who do not know of the King and His birthday.

* * *

As you see your little girl of ten or twelve enjoying education, play, the comforts of a home, the affection of parents—think for a minute of the thousands of little girls who are not older than your child, but who are already bargained for to be married.

* * *

And when your daughter in her early 'teens is being carefully shielded from every disorderly influence — remember that in Africa, little girls, no older than she is, are sitting with their own baby in their arms.

When you thus ponder over the privileges that are our portion, due to the fact that we have the knowledge of Jesus Christ, and you compare the state of these others, then heed the words of Jesus:

> "Pray ye therefore the Lord of the harvest,
> that He would send forth laborers into His
> harvest."

You ask me is the *outlook* then so very dark? We answer that the long night of heathendom is dark indeed; is cruel beyond expression. The *outlook* as viewed by the human eye is well-nigh hopeless.

But, Blessed be God, there is something greater and higher than the *outlook*. We have the *uplook*. We see Jesus, crowned Victor. We see all the purposes of God realized. We see the last of His sheep brought into the fold. We see each promise of Scripture gloriously fulfilled. We ask: "Watchman, what of the night? Watchman, what of the night?" By faith we *look up* and hear an assuring answer to our question.

"The morning cometh . . . ."